We Have This Ministry

Exposition of Second Corinthians

James Vickery
And
Martin Murphy

Second Edition

We Have This Ministry

Copyright © 2014 by James Vickery

Published by: Theocentric Publishing Group
1069A Main Street
Chipley, Florida 32428

All rights reserved. No part of this book may be reproduced or transmitted in any form or by any means without written permission of the author.

Unless otherwise noted Scripture is taken from the New King James Version. Copyright © 1979, 1980, 1982 by Thomas Nelson, Inc. Used by permission. All rights reserved.

ISBN 9780998560649

The forgotten servants who
minister in the
Body of Christ

Preface

Christianity is uniquely individual, yet collective in its scope. Every professing believer has an individual relationship with God. However, each one is distinctively related to the other, commonly referred to as the church.

Every Christian is a minister within the collective ministry of the church. It is the purpose of this book to show the relationship of the individual minister (church member) to the collective body of Christ (the church).

Paul's second letter to the Corinthians is a transparent inspired account of biblical ministry. He was a true minister to the church, not as a paid professional, but as an individual who served in the kingdom of God. Paul's work as an individual minister ought to be like a flagship for every individual Christian. This book is an exposition of the Paul's second letter to the Corinthians with a focus on the ministry of the church. If there is any redundancy, it is intentional to show that every Christian is a minister. Your ministry is to serve the Lord faithfully. Read the Scripture reference at the beginning of each chapter.

Table of Contents

1. Ministry of a Minister 1
2. Trustworthy Minister 7
3. Ministry of Love and Sorrow 13
4. Ministry of Preaching 19
5. An Effective Minister 27
6. Character of a True Minister 35
7. Ministers are Reformers 45
8. Reality Ministry 51
9. Life, Death, and Judgment 57
10. Reunion Ministry 65
11. Ministry After Reconciliation 71
12. Complex Ministry 77
13. Minister to One Another 83
14. Liberal Ministry Needed 89
15. Stewardship by Comparison 95
16. Stewardship is Honorable 101
17. How Much is Enough? 107
18. Christian Worldview Ministry 111
19. Ministry by Comparison 117
20. Image is not Everything 121
21. Earthly Man with a Heavenly Purpose 125

22 Work of a Minister 129
23 Ministry of Love and Peace 133
24 Reformation Ministry 139

1   Ministry of a Minister

2 Corinthians 1:1-11

Paul's letters to the Corinthian Church are particularly important to the modern church. They reveal the life and heartbeat of a church under the ministry of a godly apostle. Paul does not hide the fact that Corinth was a troubled church. Paul's second letter to the Corinthians describes personalities in conflict. The converted sinners at Corinth disregarded godly principles. Some of the Corinthian Christians apparently forgot the purpose, mission, and ministry of the church. The purpose of the church is to worship God (Luke 4:8). In the modern church, man-centered self-worship has replaced God-centered divine worship. The mission of the church is to make disciples and teach the whole counsel of God (Matthew 28:19-20). The ministry of the church is the building up of the body of Christ so the purpose and mission will be complete (Ephesians 4:11-16). Paul's second letter to the Corinthians will help Christians understand the ministry of a minister.

The ministry of pastors/teachers is to equip the church (the saints of God) "for the work of ministry..." (Ephesians 4:12). God never intended the gifted pastor or teacher to do all the work of ministry. The pastor's gift is that of equipping or preparing every member in the church for ministry (service). The pastor prepares the members to serve Christ and bring the church to maturity. A mature church is not one that has a few people who grow up spiritually. Everyone in the church has the responsibility to grow up spiritually.

Jesus Christ called the apostle Paul to the rigorous life of an evangelist, church planter, pastor, theologian, and teacher. In summary, those titles represent Paul's work as a minister. In the common use of religious jargon today, it is often said, that a religious leader such as a pastor is "the minister."

1 Ministry of a Minister

In the New Testament, ministers are not nearly as narrowly focused as we think in contemporary church life. For instance, in the New Testament angels are referred to as ministers. Deacons were referred to as ministers. The New Testament reveals many other people with many different responsibilities were called ministers.

Christians should be very careful how they use the word minister. For example, if you attended a social gathering where international diplomatic representatives were present and you used the word minister, they probably would not think you intended to address a member of the clergy. In many European countries a minister is one who has been given authority by the state to administer or serve as an envoy for that state.

Paul was a minister in the sense that the Bible describes a minister. Paul used the Greek word that is translated "minister" or "ministry" eighteen times in his second letter to the Corinthians. Paul wanted to serve the Corinthians, because he wanted the Corinthians to mature in the faith. The word minister and ministry are translated from the Greek word in the New Testament, *diakonos*, which is also translated servant, deacon, or minister. Paul devoted his life serving the Lord which was his ministry to the church.

The modern church often views the pastor as the minister. Since the minister is a servant, in a small church the congregation may take pride in having a pastor that serves like a servant. In a large mega-church, many members would be insulted if their celebrity pastor was also known as their servant. Although Paul was an apostle, he was a minister. Although the pastor has a unique call, he is a minister.

Every person belonging to the church of Jesus Christ is a minister. Every Christian brother or sister in Christ, is a minister. The biblical minister is one who serves in the church of the Lord Jesus Christ. God has called every Christian to minister. Every Christian is called to perform works of service in the kingdom of God. There are many ways to serve in the kingdom of God.

Ministers may provide personal help for others in the kingdom of God. Other times a minister may provide a wider service such as providing benevolence through the church to Christians in need.

Ministers in the church serve in the church faithfully assuming a servant role although they may serve as leaders in the church. For instance, it is possible to be an elder (one who rules) and serve humbly with total dependence on the Word and Spirit as the source of his strength and endurance. Every Christian is a minister in the biblical sense. The theme of this exposition from Second Corinthians will be the ministry of a minister.

Paul, the apostle, was a minister to several churches during his lifetime. One of those churches was located at Corinth. It was an old city that had been destroyed in 144 B. C., but resettled in 44 B. C. The old city of Corinth had a reputation for wealth and the new city wanted to become like the old city, wealthy and have prestige throughout the region. As in any society that desires wealth and prestige as their gods, there are men of pomp, self-love and elitism.

The Bible leaves no doubt that there were high class people in the church (Acts 18:8; 1 Corinthians 1:14; Romans 16:23). However, there were serious problems at the church in Corinth. A cursory reading of First Corinthians will reveal the problems at Corinth.

God provided Corinth with a minister and his name was Paul. He was the kind of minister who could teach and relate biblical truth to the practical situation and problems in Corinth. The apostle Paul was diligent and responsible as a pastor. He knew how to be gentle and tender with those growing up in the faith, but he also knew how to be strong and stern. Paul was a man marked by God to be a servant and to make it more emphatic, a servant minister to the church at Corinth.

Paul greets the church at Corinth by acknowledging his praise and reverence to God. He submits to his role as a minister and indicates it is the will of God that brings Paul to write the letter to the church at Corinth. The theme in the first few verses of this letter is suffering, but a humble servant of God will always acknowledge that God's will is sovereign and worthy of praise.

Paul's praise to God in light of the extenuating circumstances is remarkable. The gravity of Paul's words reveals the seriousness of the situation. Paul's situation was acute and apparently Paul thought death was near. I am not sure what event Paul had in mind. I expect it was a series of events during the time that Paul was under persecution by the angels of Satan. When persecution comes to Christians, they tend to experience depression and anxiety.

How should a Christian counteract depression and anxiety which results from suffering for the kingdom of God? By offering praise to God! The church will find comfort in suffering if she cries out like Paul, "Blessed be the God and Father of our Lord Jesus Christ" (2 Corinthians 1:3). Reverence and gratitude to God is how Christians should respond to the God of all comfort.

Suffering is a part of the Christian life. Paul told Timothy, "Do not be ashamed of the testimony of our Lord, nor of me His prisoner, but share with me in the sufferings for the gospel... ." (2 Timothy 1:8) and, "all who desire to live godly in Christ will suffer persecution" (2 Timothy 3:8).

Christians are targets for Satan and all his followers. Just as Satan is a continual enemy of Christ, so wicked men will persecute godly men. If Christians outwardly demonstrate their desire to follow Christ, ungodly men will use any method to persecute them. The Word of God leaves no doubt that evil and deceitful men and women will grow worse and worse in their attack against Christians.

When suffering for the kingdom of God comes to Christians, they should find comfort through Christ. Too often Christians trust in their own strength and abilities. Paul says no! Even if you face death, you should not trust in yourself, but in God who raises the dead.

If suffering leads to death, as Paul anticipated, the need is not just comfort, but deliverance. An implicit confidence in God's power to deliver us from this world into the New Heavens and New Earth is insufficient. It requires explicit confidence in God's power that He is able to raise the dead.

During the most severe testing, when it seems that suffering for Christ is humanly impossible to cope with, then we should always remember that our consolation abounds through Christ and that God will most certainly deliver us from death.

Scripture is a fully inspired record of God's gracious acts of deliverance. The greatest act of all is our deliverance from sin through the atoning death of the Lord Jesus Christ.

I cannot help but think that Paul had one of the many Psalms in mind when he wrote the Corinthian Church. When his enemies persecuted the Psalmist, he went to the Lord regularly to find comfort and consolation. The Psalmist said, "This is my comfort in my affliction, for Your word has given me life" (Psalm 119:50). Paul's confidence in God's power to comfort and deliver is certain, but Paul also instructs the Christians at Corinth to pray. Prayer is the means by which everyone in the church, whether poor or rich, ignorant or educated, may minister together for those who are suffering as ministers in the church. God has called every Christian to minister according to God's gift.

The ministry of mercy and comfort is a gift from God. Every Christian has the gift to show mercy to brothers and sisters in distress. Every Christian has the gift to comfort brothers and sisters in Christ who suffer physical maladies and the sinful feeling of spiritual emptiness. Your ministry may be a smile, a kind word, a helping hand, or any service to the child of God. You are a minister and you have a ministry.

2 Trustworthy Minister

2 Corinthians 1:12-22

The word minister and ministry conjure up all kinds of delusions because the word is often misused. The pastor of a local church is also referred to as the minister. In those terms, the word minister becomes a title or position of authority over the affairs of the church. The apostle Paul was a minister because he served the church. The minister serves; therefore, he will always have a ministry or a service to perform. The minister is a humble servant. Although Paul was an apostle, he was also, "a bondservant of Jesus Christ, called to be an apostle, separated to the gospel of God" (Romans 1:1). Paul referred to himself as a "bondservant" translated from the Greek word *doulos,* also translated "slave." In his service to Christ, Paul was a servant to the church. However, Paul's ministry to the church at Corinth was under attack.

> For such are false apostles, deceitful workers, transforming themselves into apostles of Christ. And no wonder! For Satan himself transforms himself into an angel of light. Therefore, it is no great thing if his ministers also transform themselves into ministers of righteousness, whose end will be according to their works. (2 Corinthians 11:13-15)

Paul's letter to the Corinthian church begins with a defense of his ministry. It was necessary because there was a conflict between ministers. Paul was a servant to the church at Corinth, yet he had become the target of criticism. The letter does not say who his critics are, but obviously, Paul writes as if the congregation at Corinth knows who they are.

2 Trustworthy Minister

Paul's ministry to the Corinthian church required him to defend his ministry. The false ministers criticized Paul. It is not an easy or comfortable way to handle criticism. Sometimes the criticism is noisy and divisive, yet without any substance. Sometimes it is best just to ignore the criticism, commit it to the Lord, and carry on with ministry. Other times it is necessary to defend the truth of the gospel against the attack. Paul's purpose of exposing the false ministers was to vindicate the righteous of Christ. Truthfulness was Paul's ultimate motive, and his testimony for Christ was faithful with the Word of God.

Paul's ministry was a Christ centered ministry. Paul's testimony was explained in terms of "a fragrance of Christ to God among those who are being saved" (2 Corinthians 2:15). "We preach Christ crucified" (1 Corinthians 1:23). The capstone of his ministry to the Corinthians was single minded. "For I determined to know nothing among you except Jesus Christ" (1 Corinthians 2:2).

The false ministers in Corinth tried to make mockery of Paul's ministry. The allegation was that he had promised to visit the church at Corinth, but had changed his plans. The change of plans was better for the Corinthians, but those who opposed his ministry used his change in travel plans against him. This may appear as an insignificant allegation, but it was the intention of Paul's opposition to accuse him of something that would get the attention of the congregation. Therefore, Paul was accused of not being trustworthy.

Paul, faithful minister of Jesus Christ, defended his ministry. Paul had to confront those in Corinth who had given their allegiance to the false apostles, because his pastoral ministry caused him to love the souls in the Corinthian Church. Paul challenged the people at Corinth to consider and decide whether Paul was a true apostle. Since Paul was the true apostle, those who stood in opposition to him would be proved false apostles. Paul makes his case loud and clear to the Corinthian Church without wavering and without ambiguity. There was no straddling the fence with Paul. His personal integrity as a minister was at stake. Everyone in the church should be concerned about personal integrity, because everyone who professes Christ is a minister and has a ministry in the church.

When your trustworthiness as a minister is questioned what should you do? Paul used a rhetorical question to defend his trustworthiness. Paul's question to the congregation was, "are my decisions according to the flesh"? (2 Corinthians 1:17). To put it another way, "do I minister to you, for your salvation, according to the ways of the world"? Every Christian makes decisions and plans, but the question is, "what is the basis for the decision or the plan." There are several questions implied in Paul's defense.

> Does my worldly wisdom lead to yes, yes and no, no at the same time?
>
> Do I say yes and no at the same time in reference to the same subject?
>
> Is this a contradiction and therefore are these words from the Father of deception?

Paul answers his own rhetorical question. "But as God is faithful, our word to you was not yes and no" (2 Corinthians 1:18). Paul's ministry was not filled with confusion, ambiguity, and contradiction. Christians have the Holy Spirit to illumine their minds to the truth found in the Word of God.

Christians should formulate a world and life view based on the Word of God and its illumination by the power of the Holy Spirit. Dr. J. P. Moreland explains the nature of a worldview:

> A person's worldview contains two important features. First, it includes the set of beliefs the person accepts, especially those about important matters such as reality, God, value, knowledge, and so on...[and] a worldview

includes the rational structure that occurs among the set of beliefs that constitute it. (*Kingdom Triangle*, by J. P. Moreland, p. 33)

Christians under the influence of the deceitful tricks of the Devil will have a worldview that is yes and no at the same time. For instance, a professing Christian may say, "yes, I believe in the sovereignty of God to one person and on another occasion say, no, I do not believe in the sovereignty of God." The problem is a lack of integrity. When people speak in contradictory terms and when they say one thing to one person and something different to another, there is sufficient reason not to trust that person.

Integrity is essential if Christians expect to be effective ministers for Christ in a postmodern culture. If Christians try to answer truth claims with a mixture of positive and negative answers, the witness of Christ has been destroyed. The question of trust is serious for every servant of Christ and every ministry in the church.

Paul gives the Corinthian Church the reason he could be trusted. "But as God is faithful, our word to you was not Yes and No" (2 Corinthians 1:18). God gave Paul the Word of God and the Word of God can be trusted. The Corinthians already knew that God could be trusted as Paul wrote in his first letter to the Corinthians. "God is faithful, by whom you were called into the fellowship of His Son, Jesus Christ our Lord" (1 Corinthians 1:9). Paul said it best in his letter to the Roman church. "Indeed, let God be true but every man a liar" (Romans 3:4). "Let God be true" is the foundation for the Word of God.

God is sovereign and he cannot and will not make any mistakes. Serving a sovereign God requires every servant in the church to embrace the full counsel of God. God's truth is a ministry for every Christian. The ministry of truth is reflected in the integrity of a person's character and will be reflected in his or her conduct.

Paul's letter to the Corinthians not only conveys the hope of a temporary solution to the problem, but also actually expects the Corinthians to come to their senses (2 Corinthians 1:13-14). Paul expected his ministry to continue in his absence.

Paul's earnest desire leads him to boast about this whole situation. Since boastfulness is not considered a Christian virtue, it is necessary to examine what Paul means, "to boast." Paul used this word 14 times in his second letter to the Corinthians. The frequency of his use of the word shows that Paul is constantly on the defense against those who oppose his ministry. Paul's boast is not in his own self-centered ego or his self-centered efforts, but his boast is in God's grace.

> If he boasts of his own behavior (2 Corinthians 1;12; cf. Galatians 6:4; James 3:14), he should do so only in so far as his life is lived in dependence on God and in responsibility to him" (*The New International Dictionary of New Testament Theology*, vol. 1, p. 229).

It was by the grace of God that Paul had a clear conscience (2 Corinthians 1:12). He put God at the center of his ministry because Paul knew the conscience is not trustworthy, because the conscience is under the power of sin. The conscience bears witness with the moral awareness of the mind. Paul's conscience was controlled by the Word of God and illumined by the Holy Spirit. Paul's self-awareness of the knowing mind and acting will was dependent on the Word of God, which means that Paul's conscience testified of his conduct before the Corinthians.

> For though we walk in the flesh, we do not war according to the flesh. For the weapons of our warfare are not carnal but mighty in God for pulling down strongholds, casting down arguments and every high thing that exalts itself against the knowledge of God, bringing every

thought into captivity to the obedience of Christ. (2 Corinthians 10:3-5)

Paul explained that holiness and sincerity had characterized his relations with the Corinthians. His ministry was trustworthy because the Word of God was trustworthy. A godly ministry will, by necessity, have a trustworthy minister. If Christians believe this portion of the Word of God, it should cause them to dig deeply into their souls and search every crevice for breaches of trust as ministers of the gospel.

Paul told the Corinthian church "we are your boasts as you also are ours, in the day of the Lord Jesus" (2 Corinthians 1:14). Boasting in human pride and arrogance is sin, but boasting in the glory of God's enabling grace to live a godly life is commendable. Paul wanted the Corinthians to rejoice in having had him as a minister, just as he would rejoice in seeing the Corinthians as fruitful ministers in the church.

Our goal as Christians should be to minister with singleness of heart and sincerity to God, so that we are known as trustworthy ministers of the gospel. John Calvin's personal motto is worthy of our attention: "I offer my heart to you, Lord, promptly and sincerely."

3   Ministry of Love and Sorrow

2 Corinthians 1:23-2:11

Paul's conversion to Christianity was 34 or 35 A.D. He ministered in churches until around 63 A.D. The full account of Paul's itinerary and ministry is not known. The general timeline for Paul's ministry is in the New Testament. Paul's ministry to the Corinthian church is not complete with times, people and events. Paul probably visited Corinth three times during his ministry. However, it is not possible to trace the day-to-day details of his ministry. We can only trace his steps as far as we have some evidence from the Word of God. There is sufficient evidence from the book of Acts and first and second Corinthians to believe that Paul communicated by letter to the church at Corinth and the church or members in the church wrote to Paul.

Paul was intimately acquainted with the congregation at Corinth. Paul made an oath to let the Corinthians know the gravity and seriousness of Paul's words, "I call God as witness against my soul, that to spare you I came no more to Corinth" (2 Corinthians 1:23). This was a serious and solemn occasion, but a time that truth was important. Paul said, "I call God as witness against my life." To put it another way, if Paul is lying, God should take his life.

If Christians expect to minister to each other, the barriers must be broken down. Serving each other in the church requires more than an academic, or willy nilly attitude. Christians cannot minister to each other if either party is unapproachable. The bond of ministry is love for God and love for each other. The Spirit of God brings Christians to the point that they can think together, make decisions together, and express their affections for one another. Paul does not act as a lord over the Corinthians. Paul sees the Corinthians as "fellow workers" (2 Corinthians 1:24).

3 Ministry of Love and Sorrow

The ministry of the church is a source of joy for ministers in the church as they work together.

The apostle Paul, far from being a stuffy, narrow-minded, pompous old theologian, was to the Corinthian Church, a minister who loved the Corinthians. However, he demonstrated his tender sorrow for God's people in the Corinthian Church. The ministry of love and sorrow weighed heavily on the mind of the apostle Paul as he wrote the Corinthians.

The ministry of love and sorrow falls on the shoulders of every person in the church. Sorrow is not something Christian's desire, but sorrow is something they experience. The word sorrow in Paul's letter to the Corinthian Church is derived from a Greek word that is also translated, "painful", "grieved" or "distress." The word "sorrow" and "grief" in this text simply means "pain."

Pain is not pleasant, but it is real and Christians are the only people who can truly understand joy in the face of pain. It is a serious mistake to believe or teach that Christ's salvation removes all the pain of this life. To the contrary, life in Christ may increase our trials and even suffering for the sake of the gospel (2 Timothy 3:12).

The *Revised Standard Version Bible* translates this text using the word "pain" instead of "sorrow" or "grief." A different perspective will help Christians understand the ministry of sorrow.

> For I made up my mind not to make you another painful visit. For if I cause you pain, who is there to make me glad but the one whom I have pained? And I wrote as I did, so that when I came I might not suffer pain from those who should have made me rejoice, for I felt sure of all of you, that my joy would be the joy of you all. For I wrote you out of much affliction and anguish of heart and with many tears, not to cause you pain but to let you know the abundant love that I have for you. But if any

> one has caused pain, he has caused it not to me, but in some measure—not to put it too severely—to you all. For such a one this punishment by the majority is enough; so you should rather turn to forgive and comfort him, or he may be overwhelmed by excessive sorrow. (2 Corinthians 2:1-7, *Revised Standard Version*).

Pain, affliction, anguish, tears and sorrow filled Paul's soul. This is life in the church when sin raises its ugly head. Paul, the trustworthy minister, wisely withheld the details of the sin and who committed it. The age-old question is, "who was the sinner at Corinth?" I do not know and neither does John Calvin and a long line of other Bible scholars who contend that Paul has the incestuous relationship mentioned in 1 Corinthians 5:1 in mind when he wrote 2 Corinthians 2.

It may have been one or more of Paul's opponents at Corinth. It could be that the man committing incest was one of his opponents. I do not know and it is not critical to the interpretation of this text.

Christians look for truth principles that honor and glorify God. Truth principles from the Word of God will help Christians understand the nature of sin and how sin may be a source of pain, affliction, anguish, and tears.

The who, the how and the why of the sin involved is not the point of this text. The one who caused Paul the pain and sorrow had been punished for the unknown sin. Paul exhibits the ministry of love and sorrow.

> This punishment which was inflicted by the majority is sufficient for such a man, so that, on the contrary, you ought rather to forgive and comfort him, lest perhaps such a one be swallowed up with too much sorrow. (2 Corinthians 2:6-7)

3 Ministry of Love and Sorrow

This is a picture of parental discipline according to Christian principles. When Christians discipline their children, they must understand they are being disciplined for their sin, which is evidence of parental love for the child. It would prove the opposite of love, not to discipline the child who had sinned. The purpose of discipline is not punishment. The purpose of discipline is repentance and restoration.

Paul's affectionate love for the repentant sinner is a ministry often ignored by Christians. The word "love" is in a sad state of disrepair among Christians. Unfortunately too many Christians think of "love" in sentimental terms or having something to do with human passions. The word love must always be interpreted in the context within which it is used.

Biblically speaking, the word "love" is inseparably related to obedience and truth. The first use of the word love in the Bible is associated with obedience. "Take now your son, your only son Isaac, whom you love, and go to the land of Moriah, and offer him there as a burnt offering on one of the mountains of which I shall tell you" (Genesis 22:2). God's blessing is "in truth and love" (2 John 1:3).

The ministry of sorrow will never be complete without the ministry of love. Christians are instructed to "speak the truth in love" (Ephesians 4:15). Love is a function of the mind because truth and love are inseparably related. Love is a function of the will because obedience and love are inseparably related. Love is also a function of the affections. It is one of the basic attitudes of life. Paul wanted the Corinthians to know of his abundant love for them, even if they had caused him much pain.

Paul may have been thinking of the new commandment Jesus gave his disciples. "A new commandment I give to you, that you love one another; as I have loved you, that you also love one another" (John 13:34). Christ issued this commandment because love was a principal of His life. He was able to rebuke and correct His disciples because He loved them. Jesus taught His disciples that love must free of prejudice and He demonstrated it because, with his last breath he prayed for the ones who murdered him (Luke 23:34).

Paul could speak of his abundant love for the Corinthians because his ministry of love and sorrow was a way of life. If Christians follow Paul's experience, they will forgive the offending brethren, because the Corinthian Church had forgiven them. Love is the necessary ingredient for forgiveness.

When Christians do all that is within their ability, they must not forget that Satan is out to destroy the church. The apostle Paul reminds the church not to be ignorant of Satan's schemes. Although Satan is a finite being, we must not forget that Satan's powers of intelligence and ability to deceive people is great beyond our imagination. Satan would deceive us to believe that we must not forgive, that love is a worldly sensation, and that pain is a result of misguided religious conviction. Satan will try to confuse and frustrate the ministry of love and sorrow. God's people must resist the devil and minister with godly biblical love.

Ministry in the church often begins with sorrow because it is real. However, godly comfort will overcome the sorrow for those who belong to Jesus Christ. Biblical love is necessary, but sentimental unbiblical love will only bring more pain. The capstone of this exposition is that forgiveness must follow repentance in the ministry of love and sorrow.

4 Ministry of Preaching

2 Corinthians 2:12-17

The ministry of preaching may sound like a one man show. More often than not, sermons are "performed" by silver tongue talkers, commonly known as preachers. The sermon has become an idol for many pastors/preachers. The ministry of preaching has turned into an inspirational pep talk. Like any other ministry in the church, preaching is a ministry for everyone in the congregation. For the preacher, it is a duty appointed by God. For the elders, it is a ministry of holding the preacher accountable. For the congregation, it is a ministry of engagement and responsibility. The *Westminster Larger Catechism* has a question and answer that reveals the ministry of preaching for everyone in the congregation.

> Question 160. What is required of those that hear the Word preached?
>
> Answer: It is required of those that hear the Word preached, that they attend upon it with diligence, preparation, and prayer; examine what they hear by the Scriptures; receive the truth with faith, love, meekness, and readiness of mind, as the Word of God; meditate, and confer of it; hide it in their hearts, and bring froth the fruit of it in their lives.

After hearing the preaching of the Word of God, Christians must meditate on it and make sure that the sermon was God-centered doctrine, not man-made doctrine. The ministry of preaching will have a profound effect on understanding biblical theology. A biblical preaching ministry will help Christians formulate a godly worldview.

4 Ministry of Preaching

Although the church has failed to follow a biblically defined mission and ministry, the lack of sound preaching is at the forefront of the failure. The mission of the church is to make disciples. The ministry of the church is the service necessary to fulfill the mission of the church. Preaching according to the principles in Scripture will give life to the mission and ministry of the church (Ezekiel 33:1-11; John 8:47; 2 Timothy 4:1-5; 2 Corinthians 2:12-17).

Preaching with purpose is at the heart of the mission and ministry of the church. Let me preface everything I say with this qualification. The word "preach" or "preaching" must take every word in the Bible into consideration. The great challenge today is to preach the full counsel of God.

Preaching is not just an evangelistic enterprise. There is a redemptive purpose in preaching, but preaching is much more than telling people about God's saving grace. An often used expression for those who have a dislike for the full counsel of God is, "Don't give me theology, just give me Jesus." That may sound concise and cute, but it is a deadly error. The question is which Jesus is the real Jesus? Is it the Jesus, who is the human man with the divine idea? That is the teaching of Christian Science. Is it Jesus the first son that Jehovah God brought forth? That is the teaching of the Jehovah Witness organization. Is it the Jesus that was just like any other human except without original sin? That is the teaching of the Unification Church. They all give you Jesus, but they deny the deity of Jesus. It would take an entire book to discover the nature and character of Jesus Christ.

The short version may be described as preaching theology is out and preaching "according to their own desires" is the prevailing attitude in Western Christianity (2 Timothy 4:3). Preaching theology is out and preaching what people want to hear is in. The church growth movement popularized in the 1980's and the emergent church movement around the turn of the century took the psychology of Abraham Maslow's hierarchy of needs and created the preaching of "felt needs." Sad to say, too many ministers place a low priority toward preaching. The purpose for preaching is to make known the gospel of the kingdom of Jesus Christ and preaching sound doctrine from the full counsel of God.

Consulting the full counsel of God will reveal the account of Paul on his second missionary journey and the Macedonian call. In God's providence, Paul was not able to go into Asia. Paul went to Troas and there had a vision that compelled him to go to Macedonia. Paul's purpose was to preach the Gospel of the kingdom of Jesus Christ. Paul not only preached with purpose, but God planned the preaching opportunities (2 Corinthians 2:12). Paul went to Troas to preach, but God had plans for Paul to preach in another place. The Bible explains how "a door was opened to me." The grammar makes it clear; Paul did not use church politics nor depend on pulpit committees to move to Macedonia. The same agent who issued the mandate to preach is the same agent who gave the opportunity. The Lord commanded that he preach and the Lord gave the opportunity. Preachers and elders must cut out playing church politics and seek the will of God according to scriptural principles and God's providence.

Paul spoke in terms of sense perception when he described his preaching ministry. He said, "We are to God the fragrance of Christ." To put this in lucid terms, "We are to God an aroma of Christ." His preaching, and all preaching for that matter, is offered to God as the primary object. As the ultimate Judge of all things God will determine the worth of the preaching. People in a congregation may find the preaching acceptable or even "heart moving", but if God does not find it acceptable, it has no worth.

The text in Ezekiel chapter thirty three is a corollary to Paul's ministry of preaching.

> Again the word of the LORD came to me, saying, "Son of man, speak to the children of your people, and say to them: 'When I bring the sword upon a land, and the

people of the land take a man from their territory and make him their watchman, when he sees the sword coming upon the land, if he blows the trumpet and warns the people, then whoever hears the sound of the trumpet and does not take warning, if the sword comes and takes him away, his blood shall be on his own head. He heard the sound of the trumpet, but did not take warning; his blood shall be upon himself. But he who takes warning will save his life. But if the watchman sees the sword coming and does not blow the trumpet, and the people are not warned, and the sword comes and takes any person from among them, he is taken away in his iniquity; but his blood I will require at the watchman's hand. "So you, son of man: I have made you a watchman for the house of Israel; therefore you shall hear a word from My mouth and warn them for Me. When I say to the wicked, 'O wicked man, you shall surely die!' and you do not speak to warn the wicked from his way, that wicked man shall die in his iniquity; but his blood I will require at your hand. Nevertheless if you warn the wicked to turn from his way, and he does not turn from his way, he shall die in his iniquity; but you have delivered your soul. (Ezekiel 33:1-9)

The Old Testament watchman may serve in one of several capacities. Watchmen were stationed on city walls so they could alert the city if hostile action threatened the city. Watchmen were also appointed to watch over fields and vineyards during the time of harvest. The prophets used the term "watchman" as a metaphor to describe a prophet as a watchman for God. It was the duty of the watchman to announce to the people of God either good news or impending doom as the case may be.

God commissioned the prophet Ezekiel as a watchman for the house of Israel. Ezekiel had already been taken captive to Babylon and apparently ministered to a group of Jewish captives by the River Chebar. You might call them the underground church of the Old Testament. Ezekiel spoke words of hope concerning the restoration of the Old Testament saints to the land of their forefathers. Ezekiel also spoke words of judgment to the Old Testament saints in exile. His warning was, "turn now to the Lord, because God delighted in those who turned from sin."

Ezekiel's words are as fresh as the morning news paper and Christians need to hear afresh the Word of God delivered from the mouthpiece of God. If the minister neglects to warn the people we find that the sinner's blood will be required at the minister's hand. However, if the people do not take heed to the Word of God their blood will be on their own shoulders.

The doctrine of distinctions is like the task of a taxonomist; His responsibility is to classify objects. Paul classifies the human race into two categories, the saved and the unsaved. Therefore, the preaching ministry has God as its object and people who are saved and unsaved as its audience.

The doctrine of salvation is in dispute because the distinctions have created vast chasms in the modern church. Paul said the aroma of Christ is "among those who are being saved and among those who are perishing" (2 Corinthians 2:15). Who is responsible for the salvation of a soul? There are three negatives to tie together the answer.

Not the Christian - he is being saved.

Not the preacher - He does not have the ability to save a soul from damnation.

Not the church - It has not been charged with the responsibility to save souls.

Salvation is from God and He alone is responsible for the salvation of souls. It is the responsibility of the individual sinner to believe on the Lord Jesus Christ for the forgiveness of sins.

Then the saved sinner will find preaching an eternal blessing. It will be a fragrance of life.

The unsaved sinner finds preaching bitter, because the Word of God warns the sinner. Paul's warning to the unsaved was, "we are a fragrance of Christ to God among those who are perishing" (2 Corinthians 2:15). The Word of God is disgusting to unsaved sinners. Paul had already warned the Corinthians. "For the message of the cross is foolishness to those who are perishing, but to us who are being saved it is the power of God" (1 Corinthians 1:18).

The ministry of preaching produces the smell of life to some, while for others preaching produces the smell of death. The following questions will bring this closer to home. Do you love the preaching of the Word of God and how it builds you up and strengthens your life? Do you despise the preaching of the Word of God and how it deals with sin in your life? The rebellious human heart will hear one thing, but the heart empowered by the Spirit will hear something else, from the same gospel.

The ministry of preaching will affect every person that professes faith and finds his or her place in the family of God. The sad truth is that preaching the Word of God is either true preaching or false preaching. Paul referred to the dilemma in his day. "For we are not, as so many, peddling the word of God" (2 Corinthians 2:17). This is not a meandering reference by the apostle. To the Galatian Church he wrote, "if any man is preaching to you a gospel contrary to that which you received, let him be accursed" (Galatians 1:9). To the Philippian Church he wrote, "Some to be sure, are preaching Christ even from envy and strife, but some also from good will" (Philippians 1:15).

The English word "peddle" is derived from the Greek word *kapalos*. The word referred to a shyster peddling his wares similar to the old west medicine doctor. "The word comes to mean almost adulterate" (*The Greek-English Lexicon of the New Testament and Other Early Christians Literature*, The University of Chicago Press). This type of preaching was literally fake. False preaching will lead to the road of despair. The pew needs to awaken out of its slumber. God has given the church pastors and teachers to preach the full counsel of God so the church will be blessed forever.

The true preaching of the Word of God will have a remarkable effect on all who hear it. Anytime someone hears the true preaching of the full counsel of God, the metaphor Paul used in 2 Corinthians 2:14-16 ought to come to mind. This metaphor describes a Roman triumphal procession as the general leads his captives before the crowd of onlookers. Incense is burnt to the gods, but the smell flows to the nostrils of the enemy as well as the victors. The same incense smells radically different to the captured slaves than to the victors.

We were once God's enemies, but God has taken us captive. While we were enemies the preaching of the Word of God had an awful aroma. But now that God has taken us captive rather than having a bad smell, the Word of God has a sweet aroma. Paul spoke in terms of "every place" reminding the reader that the gospel of the kingdom of Christ is ever advancing. There is progress in God's redemptive plan. It was evident in the early church and still is today. "So the churches were strengthened in the faith, and increased in number daily" (Acts 16:5).

Preaching a false gospel will produce false converts. False converts fill the church and cause great damage to the church, but false converts perish in the end. Preaching a true gospel will produce true converts. True converts are a blessing to the church; and they will be with God forever.

5 An Effective Minister

2 Corinthians 3:1-18

The church consists of professing believers and their children. They are ministers in the sense that they perform works of service in the kingdom of God. Believers minister in a servant role according to God's call on his or her life. Each one with his or her particular gift contributes to the kingdom of Christ, sometimes in a local church and at other times serves the church on a wider scale.

Paul's ministry to the church at Corinth was in the context of a large cosmopolitan city for that time in the history of the world. Corinth was a banking center with all the wealth and prosperity that goes along with financial success. Religious life was like many other Mediterranean cities. The Doric Temple was located at Corinth. In it was an ornamental fountain in honor of Peseidon and Aphrodite, the Greek goddess of life, beauty and passion whom the Romans called Venus. Corinth could boast of its epicurean world and life view, much like America can boast of its postmodern world and life view. Corinth pretended to seek wisdom in the popular culture of its day, a notion not much different than modern times. In the middle of this sophisticated society, one could find moral corruption as common as it is in America. It was in this socio-economic, morally corrupt, religious setting that the apostle Paul gathered a few people together and started a church.

Paul spent one and a half years as the evangelist, church planter and pastor at Corinth. Probably five years lapsed before he wrote second Corinthians. Division, factions, strife and sorrow was commonplace in the congregation by the time Paul wrote second Corinthians. Paul was a minister among and to this kind of situation in the church. Ministry will always find socio-economic class distinctions, moral corruption, and religious convictions. Paul's first ministry to the Corinthians was the announcement of the gospel. The entire Bible reveals the message of salvation, implicitly in the Old Testament and explicitly in the New Testament. Every believer has heard the gospel message and believed it. Their duty as an effective minister is to share the good news with unbelievers.

Letters of commendation have been used through the centuries to introduce and commend one party to another. Paul's opponents at Corinth had probably brought letters of commendation. Paul's opponents may also have convinced the Corinthians that the apostle Paul and his companions were not credible ministers, because they did not have letters of commendation. Paul was straight to the point when he asked the Corinthians: "do we need, as some others, letters of commendation?" Paul was a minister of the gospel; a minister called by God, an effective minister. Paul had already said, "For we are not, as so many, peddling the Word of God" (2 Corinthians 2:17). Paul did not peddle the Word of God, because as an effective minister he simply gave them the gospel message.

Paul's gospel message was, "God demonstrates His own love toward us, in that while we were still sinners, Christ died for us" (Romans 5:8). He gave the Corinthians the same essential message, but couched in different terms. "For I delivered to you first of all that which I also received; that Christ died for our sins according to the Scriptures and that He was buried and that He rose again the third day according to the Scriptures..." (1 Corinthians 15:3ff).

The modern gospel is "believe, because God has a wonderful plan for your life" or some similar composition. It is contrary to the Word of God. The gospel is not needed until the unbeliever confesses that he or she is a sinner, an ungodly lawbreaker and in need of God's forgiveness. The good news is that Christ died to save His people (Matthew 1:21).

When Christians say "man is a sinner", do they realize what that means? Paul says it is "the ministry of death" (2

Corinthians 3:7), but at the same time he says it is a glorious ministry. The Old Covenant is a glorious ministry because the law is the way that man knows he is eternally condemned. The Old Covenant was glorious because without it there is no need for the gospel. Even without the gospel, the Old Covenant is glorious because God is shown to be almighty, sovereign, and holy in all His ways.

If the Old Covenant was glorious, the New Covenant was exceedingly more glorious. The Old Covenant declares the penalty of sin brings death. The New Covenant teaches Christ paid the penalty for the sins of those whom God has called to Himself.

Jeremiah preached the New Covenant was the manifestation of God's redeeming grace. A brief summary of Jeremiah's prophesy is necessary to understand Paul's reference to the New Covenant.

> Behold, the days are coming, says the LORD, when I will make a new covenant with the house of Israel and with the house of Judah — not according to the covenant that I made with their fathers in the day that I took them by the hand to lead them out of the land of Egypt, My covenant which they broke, though I was a husband to them, says the LORD. But this is the covenant that I will make with the house of Israel after those days, says the LORD: I will put My law in their minds, and write it on their hearts; and I will be their God, and they shall be My people. (Jeremiah 31:31-33)

The prophet, Jeremiah, must have been a godly, but fearless man to stand in the face of the religious hypocrites in Jerusalem. Jeremiah was thought to be a weeping prophet. He should be called the broken hearted prophet. He was weeping for the sins of God's covenant people. Jeremiah spent his whole prophetic ministry in Jerusalem until the fall of Jerusalem in 586

B. C. and Jeremiah saw the imminent destruction of Jerusalem. Repeatedly, Jeremiah prophesied the destruction of Jerusalem. "This is the city to be punished. She is full of oppression in her midst" (Jeremiah 6:6). Jeremiah's prophesy was specific and scathing. "And the Chaldeans shall come back and fight against this city, and take it and burn it with fire" (Jeremiah 37:8).

These prophecies are heart breaking. These prophecies were directed to the religious people of Israel, the covenant people of God. Today the covenant people of God are referred to as the church. In contrast to these prophecies of destruction, God had a plan to save His people. His plan is known as the "covenant of redemption." The covenant of redemption was the eternal agreement in which God the Father would call His people for His eternal glory. God the Son agreed to redeem those whom God called, after they had fallen, and God the Holy Spirit agreed to apply the work of Christ to God's covenant people.

The covenant of redemption is an eternal covenant where Jesus Christ binds Himself to redeem God's covenant people. "All that the Father gives Me will come to Me, and the one who comes to Me I will by no means cast out. For I have come down from heaven, not to do My own will, but the will of Him who sent Me" (John 6:37-38).

God's covenant of redemption is eternal, but God fulfills his promise to redeem His people through various covenants throughout human history. These various biblical covenants abound with God's grace, so we refer to God's covenant of grace.

The covenant God made with Abraham was the manifestation of the formal institution of God's covenant of grace for His people. God's covenant promise to Abraham was to make a great nation (Genesis 12:3). Read Genesis 15 for a better understanding of God's promise.

The Mosaic covenant or the covenant of law follows God's covenant with Abraham. This covenant is part of the gracious unfolding of the covenant of grace and is not contrary to grace. The law covenant that God made with Moses does not replace or change the covenant of promise God made with Abraham. The announcement of the law covenant itself begins with the reminder to the people that they have been the recipients of salvation from Egypt. "I am the LORD thy God, who brought thee out of the land of Egypt, out of the house of bondage" (Exodus 20:2).

Included in this covenant were provisions for the failure of sinners to live up to God's perfect demands. The priesthood, the tabernacle and the Levitical sacrificial system were part of God's covenant of grace. God provided the way of access to His throne room through the shed blood of the lambs of sacrifice. A sense of guilt and of the need of reconciliation was constantly kept alive by daily sacrifices, at first in the tabernacle and afterwards in the temple, and by the whole ceremonial law, which, as a wonderful system of types and shadows, perpetually pointed to the realities of the New Covenant, especially to the one all-sufficient atoning sacrifice of Christ on the cross. The eternal covenant of redemption manifested the salvation of God's people through the sacrifice of the Passover lamb and deliverance by the mighty arm of Jehovah. This sacrifice was a type of the Christ who would finally redeem His people with a once for all sacrifice of Himself.

God's promise of eternal salvation would not make much sense unless God's people had a sovereign (king) and an eternal home. The idea of kingship is significant for the Church itself, because if Christ is her King, He is the only lawgiver. It is His law that should be obeyed in all things, both in faith and in practice. If there is a King, there is a kingdom (2 Samuel 7:12-14).

God's promise to redeem His people is one continuous process through various covenants that God makes with His people. The covenants in the Old Testament show the progressive expansion of God's kingdom. The Old Testament covenants culminate in the New Covenant.

5 An Effective Minister

When the Bible speaks of Israel in Jeremiah thirty one it certainly is not limited only to the physical Israel but must also apply to the gentiles for whom Christ came and died; it is the elect who are designated as "the lost sheep of the house of Israel" (Matthew 15:24). Jesus Christ did not save the nation Israel as a political nation, but he saved His own people, His covenant people, both Jews and Gentiles. Covenant theologians understand from the full counsel of God that the New Covenant applies to the Christian Church.

God's covenant promises are perpetual. The doctrine of the New Covenant simply fulfills all the previous covenant promises in the person and work of Jesus Christ, who was to come, who is and who will be. The New Covenant brings to light the fullness of God's redemptive plan through His covenant promises. The New Covenant is a triad doctrine.

The first component is that God will put His law in their minds and write the law on their hearts. Looking back at the law covenant, we find that God externalized his law on tablets of stone for the good of His people, but in the New Covenant, it is said that God "writes the law in their minds, and their hearts" (Jeremiah 31:33). Specifically the passage teaches that the Old Covenant, which was external in nature, being written on tablets of stone, will now become internally written by the Spirit on the hearts of God's people. The prophet does not mean that the only knowledge of the law of God was written on those stone tablets prior to the fulfillment of the New Covenant. Long before Jeremiah's prophesy, the Psalmist said, "Your law is within my heart" (Psalm 40:8). The apostle Paul makes it clear that the law was written on the hearts of all men (Romans 2:14-15). What Jeremiah means is that the law of God is not a loathsome law in the New Covenant. The saints of the New Covenant have a clearer understanding of God's gracious grace by the redemptive work of the Lord Jesus Christ. Under the New Covenant, the Holy Spirit causes the believer to see the acuteness of violating God's law. Then it follows that we will see the magnified beauty of Christ, who is the keeper of the law. Under the New Covenant, God's people not only want to see the magnified beauty of Christ; they want to see Christ being formed in the soul. It is the preaching of the Word and the administration of the sacraments (baptism and Lord's Supper) that imprint the image of Christ on the heart and soul. When the Holy Spirit writes the law on the heart, the law is then loved by God's people.

The second component of the New Covenant unites God's covenant people. "No more shall every man teach his neighbor, and every man his brother, saying, Know the Lord, for they all shall know Me, from the least of them to the greatest of them..." (Jeremiah 31:34). This aspect of the New Covenant does not militate against the duty required of external religious instruction. It does mean that Gentiles and Jews alike, individually, would have immediate access to God through the Lord Jesus Christ. Under the Old Covenant, human mediation by the priest was essential for understanding ones relationship with God. Of course, that was a mere type of the ultimate Mediator, the Lord Jesus Christ.

The third component of the New Covenant was the full revelation of man's greatest need, the forgiveness of sin and sins. "I will forgive their iniquity, and their sin I will remember no more" (Jeremiah 31:34). After centuries of repeated sacrifices seeking the forgiveness of sin, God promises full and final forgiveness, a promise that required the death of God's only son, the Lord Jesus Christ.

The Mediator of the New Covenant is Jesus Christ. His blood is the basis on which the blessings of this covenant comes to the covenant people of God (Hebrews 12:24). God's covenant people serve the King as effective ministers.

The efficacious work of the Holy Spirit precedes the effective work of a minister. An effective minister will herald God's message, but he does not have the authority or power to make the message accomplish its purpose. Only the efficacious work of the Holy Spirit causes the message to accomplish its purpose. The preservation and the perpetuity of the gospel are safe and secure because of the power and ability of God working through the lives of His effective ministers. Paul said God has "made us sufficient as ministers of the New covenant."

The opponents of God's effective minister will try to trample under foot the gospel of Christ. Christians must grasp, believe, trust, and practice the foundation upon which he or she may build an effective ministry. "Not that we are sufficient of ourselves to think of anything as being from ourselves, but our sufficiency is from God" (2 Corinthians 3:5).

Has God called you to be a minister? The answer is yes, if you are a child of God. If you belong to the true and living God, He has called you not only to be a minister, but an effective minister.

6 Character of a True Minister

2 Corinthians 4:1-6

The Apostle Paul's ministry to the Corinthians was to take the role of a slave. Paul considered himself a slave to the church members at Corinth. Several translations avoid Paul's emphasis on slavery. The *New American Standard Bible* translators were courageous enough to use the word "bond-servant," which literally refers to a slave (2 Corinthians 4:5). However in Paul's first letter to the Corinthians Paul said, "I have made myself a slave to all, that I might win the more" (*New American Standard Bible*, 1 Corinthians 9:19). A slave is always a servant and Paul wants to drive that point home.

The apostle Paul understood the concept that Jesus taught so clearly in the gospel of Matthew: "whoever wished to become great among you shall be your servant, and whoever wishes to be first among you shall be your slave; just as the Son of Man did not come to be served, but to serve, and to give His life a ransom for many" (Matthew 20:26-28).

Ministry by means of servitude has Jesus Christ at the center of the doctrine. The ministry of servitude is directly connected to the doctrine of humility.

> Let this mind be in you which was also in Christ Jesus who, being in the form of God, did not consider it robbery to be equal with God, but made Himself of no reputation, taking the form of a bondservant and coming in the likeness of men. (Philippians 2:5-6)

The word "bondservant" literally refers to a "slave." A lengthy quote from the book, *The Dominant Culture: Living in the Promised Land*, will be helpful to understand slavery from a biblical perspective.

6 Character of a True Minister

The Greek word for slave is *doulos*, which signified ownership. The slave belonged to someone else. For instance in Paul's letter to the Romans he declared himself to be "a slave of Christ Jesus" (Romans 1:1). The New Kings James Version and New American Standard Bible state that Paul was a bondservant of Jesus Christ. The Greek word translated bondservant is the Greek word *doulos*. Other translations use the word servant.

Today we think of a servant as one who is paid to carry out the mundane choirs of life. We hire such a one to cook, clean the house, cut the yard, etc. The Bible had a name for the hired servant. The Greek word that describes the hired hand is *misthotos*. The Bible describes the calling of James the son of Zebedee and John his brother who were mending fish nets in these terms: "And immediately He (Jesus) called them: and they left their father Zebedee in the boat with the hired servants (*misthotos*) and went away to follow Him. Paul did not consider himself a hired servant of Jesus Christ.

There is another word used in the text of the Greek manuscript that describes a servant and that word is *therapon*. This word describes one who performs a service in the interest of public good. For instance, Hebrews 3:5 says, "Now Moses was faithful in all His house as a servant (*therapon*), for a testimony of those things which were to be spoken later. Paul was not just a public servant for the good of humanity.

There is another word used in the Greek text that describes a servant. The word is *huperetes*. This word describes one person who is subordinate to another person. Although Paul used this word to describe himself as a servant of Christ, the word is used most often to refer to officers acting submissively to his commander.

Another word translated "servant" in the New Testament is from the Greek word *diakovos*. Most often, we translate it as deacon but it is also translated servant such as when Paul describes Epaphras in Colossians 1:7. The idea is that Epaphras served in the church as a deacon in a way similar to the way a deacon would serve in the church today.

All these words except *doulos* represent a master servant relationship. There is nothing humiliating in any of these terms, but the word slave (*doulos*) is humiliating. The English words bondservant or servant in Paul's letter to the Romans takes away from the original Greek word, which is slave (*doulos*). The word *doulos* means slave. Even though a slave may achieve a high position in life such as the very responsible position held by Nehemiah or Daniel, the high position did not remove the stigma of slavery.

Paul was a Hebrew of Hebrews and a Roman Citizen. He held dual citizenship (actually triple citizenship when we consider his citizenship in heaven). A man who held his honored civil position would never have submitted himself as a slave to another human being. However, Paul was happy to be called a slave of Jesus Christ and calls himself a slave again in Philippians 1:1. Paul was happy to be called a slave to the one whom not only created him, but who redeemed him from his fallen estate and governed every action in Paul's life.

Truly, it may be said that when one is a slave of Jesus Christ, that one has the truest liberty and the highest dignity. To be a slave brings with it a sense of belonging - a sense of ownership if you don't mind. The kind of freedom sinful man seeks is an independent spirit. Sinful man says, "I want to be my own self. I want to control my own life. I reject the institution of slavery."

6 Character of a True Minister

We all have different gifts and abilities, which should be nurtured, but we too often forget that those are gifts and not self-achievements. If we could see ourselves like the apostle Paul saw himself, we would desire to be called a slave of Jesus Christ.

There is a story told about a slave who despised the thought of being owned by an Englishman. The slave said he would never obey so unworthy a master. However, after the purchase the slave learned that his New master had purchased him to give him his freedom. The poor slave was so overwhelmed by joy and gratitude, he said, "I am your slave for ever." His freedom made him a slave.

The Psalmist said it well when he said, "O Lord, truly I am Your servant; I am Your servant, the son of Your maidservant, You have loosed my bonds. I will offer to You the sacrifice of thanksgiving and will call upon the name of the Lord." (Psalm 116:16ff)

Now put yourself in the place of the Roman Christians who received Paul's letter. Rome was a cosmopolitan city that was about as wicked a place to live as any you could image today.

Edward Gibbon in his monumental *History of the Decline and Fall of the Roman Empire has* estimated that "slaves under the reign of Claudius" reached nearly one-half of the population. Others estimate that there were three slaves to every freeman. It has been said that the slaves were worse off than animals during the day in which Paul wrote his letter to the Romans. In Taylor's word on Civil Law he said: "Slaves had no head of the state, no name, no title, or register; they were not capable to being injured; they had no heirs and therefore could make no will; they were not entitled to the rights and considerations of matrimony, and they had no relief in case of adultery; they could be sold, transferred, or pawned, as goods or personal estate; they might be tortured for evidence, punished at the discretion of their lord, and even put to death by his authority." (*History of the Christian Church*, by Philip Schaff, pg. 447).

Now that you have a little history to think about, I ask you to put yourself in the place of those Roman Christians who received Paul's letter. How would you feel or think after reading the first line, "Paul a slave of Jesus Christ"? Did they ask the question "Is Paul crazy?" Who wants to be a slave? The answer is simple if we use God's definition for freedom and slavery. No one wants to be a slave unless the institution functions according to God's law. However, under God's law it is not a bad institution at all, if fact, if perfected it appears that Paul prefers biblical slavery over against secular freedom.

In his opening words to the Romans, we find that this slave was called to be an apostle. The noble call of an apostle however never preceded the real effectual call of God to bring Paul into a state of salvation. Paul properly understood his relationship to Christ in terms of freedom and slavery. "Do you not know that when you present yourselves to someone as slaves for obedience, you are slaves of the one whom you obey, either of sin resulting in death, or of obedience resulting in righteousness?" (Romans 6:16). Did Paul find freedom in slavery? The answer is a resounding yes!

Paul's parentage, birth, gifts, education and call was distinctively different that the other apostles. As I said earlier, Paul possessed dual citizenship. His rhetorical and writing skills were superior to the other apostles. His education was very different. Paul studied at the feet of the great Rabbi Gamaliel and then he studied for years after he was converted in preparation for the ministry. The other apostles had a short three-year preparation. Paul was not ignorant of his unique call for in 2 Corinthians 11:5 Paul under inspiration he said, "For I consider that I am not at all inferior to the most eminent apostles." Apparently, his position as a slave did not interfere with his high position as an apostle. (*The Dominant Culture: Living in the Promised Land*, by Martin Murphy, pg.28-32)

The apostle Paul was a man who had been given authority by Jesus Christ to serve as a minister in His church. It is for that reason that Paul was compelled to serve the church at Corinth. In the truest sense of the word, a minister in the church is a servant to the church. It logically follows then that every Christian is a minister, because the Bible commands Christians to serve one another (Galatians 5:13). Christians are ministers to the church and their duty is to serve not to be served.

The character of a true minister expresses a heart for service demonstrated by humility. The Bible speaks positively about serving with humility. The Bible also warns the true minister to avoid three pitfalls.

Do not lose heart.
Do not walk in craftiness.
Do not handle the Word of God deceitfully.

The true minister does not lose heart. Literally, Paul says, "we faint not." Remember the context in which Paul speaks to the church. One of the main reasons Paul wrote Corinthians is because his opponents came to Corinth to discredit the apostle's ministry. Paul's opponents must have caused him affliction and suffering. However, Paul did not lose heart.

The character of a true minister is such that he or she will not lose heart in the face of affliction, pain, and suffering. Self-esteem and self-confidence will not sustain you, but the Word of God will be a constant source of strength. "Likewise the Spirit also helps in our weaknesses" (Romans 8:26). Paul's gospel was the eternal truth for which no man should be ashamed. The true gospel is characteristic of a true minister. The two fit like a glove and a hand. Christians may get discouraged because they are sinners, but they should not lose heart because the gospel will prevail in the end.

An open and honest demeanor will mark the character of a true minister. The apostle said he had "renounced the hidden things of shame, not walking in craftiness nor handling the Word of God deceitfully" (2 Corinthians 4:2). Shame is a condition that often causes God's people to turn away from their ministry. It is not uncommon for professing Christians to withhold the gospel for fear of being ridiculed. There is nothing in the gospel for which a true minister should be ashamed.

The character of a true minister does not depend on craftiness or of cunning devices. Craftiness is totally out of place in Christian ministry. Christian ministry is never justified by crafty or cunning dealings. Not even to bring about what seems to be good to the one practicing the crafty deed. Paul did not practice shifty, shrewd, or slippery conduct, because Paul wanted to demonstrate honesty and integrity for the sake of the gospel. Most if not all division and strife in the church would be eliminated if the servants of Jesus Christ lived open lives and refused to stoop to the crafty cunning dealings with others in the church.

The character of a true Christian minister will not handle the Word of God deceitfully. Unfortunately, the popular notion today is a wide spread belief in the relativity of truth. It is a spreading cancer, even among Christians to believe that what is morally true for one person is not necessarily morally true for another person. True Christian ministers maintain that which is biblically and logically true. Therefore, true ministers must persuade or challenge others with the truth claims from Scripture. Truth does not come in different colors. The apostle Paul said his yes is yes and his no is no (2 Corinthians 1:18).

6 Character of a True Minister

The opponents of Jesus Christ did not believe the truth. The Lord said to the religious leaders in Jerusalem, "but because I tell the truth, you do not believe me" (John 8:45). The age-old question is this: Why do people reject truth? One reason is that men tend to determine what is true and what is not true by private self-judgment, rather than submitting to an ultimate authority. Paul responds by saying, "we commend ourselves to every man's conscience in the sight of God" (2 Corinthians 4:2).

False teachers pull the wool over the eyes of those who are perishing. On the contrary, the true Christian minister says, "For we are to God the fragrance of Christ among those who are being saved and among those who are perishing" (2 Corinthians 2:15). The gospel is hidden, not because of the true character of the minister of the gospel, but because the god of this age has blinded the minds of those who do not believe the gospel. "The god of this world has blinded the minds of those who do not believe" (2 Corinthians 4:4). Unbelievers cannot see the light of the gospel. That does not mean that unbelievers do not have some apprehension of truth. However, an unbeliever will not desire gospel truth.

Paul says if our gospel is veiled, it is veiled to those who are perishing. Certainly, the Bible teaches that Satan will use everything at his disposal to deceive people and hide the gospel. Sometimes Satan will use the things of this world to distract people from the gospel. Other times he will use the troubles of this world to hide the gospel. Satan will use every diversion possible to get control of the minds of those who are perishing in their sin and sins. If Satan can control the mind, the gospel will remain undercover.

Satan may cause blindness, but God gives light to His own. When God makes the light shine in the heart, then the mind has the knowledge of the glory of God. Without being redundant, let me say that unbelievers have knowledge of God, but they don't like what they know. True Christian ministers have the knowledge of the glory of God and they love what they know.

God said let there be light. That act of God in creation was miraculous and supernatural, but no more so than God giving the light of the knowledge of the glory of God to His own people. The character of a true minister will be shaped as God's light shines into the sinful dark heart. The true minister stands ready, not with a faint heart, but with a heart filled with the love of God, ready to commend the gospel and his or her life in the sight of God.

7   Ministers are Reformers

2 Corinthians 4:7-15

A minister is one who serves God, but what is a "reformer" and what does he or she do? The writer of Hebrews used the word reformation to explain the change from the Old Covenant ministry in temple worship to the New Covenant ministry of worship (Hebrews 9:10). God commanded Jeremiah to warn the people to reform themselves.

> Thus says the LORD, 'Behold, I am fashioning calamity against you and devising a plan against you. Oh turn back, each of you from his evil way, and reform your ways and your deeds"' (Jeremiah 18:11).

Reformation is a call to God's people to make corrections to the way they think and act.

Reformation is a way of life for Christians. Reformation begins when individual Christians realize the need to discover or re-discover the true teaching of the full counsel of God. It is the daily renewal of the soul according to the Word of God by the power of the Holy Spirit. Reformation was part of the life of Moses, Hezekiah, Josiah, Ezra/Nehemiah and especially during the earthly life of Jesus. Paul's ministry to the Corinthian Church was a ministry of reformation. He wanted them to discover from the Word of God, the error of their ways. His ministry was to set them on the right course.

After the death of the last apostle, the church experienced the rapid spread of false teachers and false doctrine, because the church collectively did not seek reformation. From the beginning of the Christian empire to the sixteenth century, the church failed to preach and pray for reformation. Martin Luther came to realize that the church had departed from the clear teaching of the Word of God.

At first the church ignored Luther, but quickly he became known as a troublemaker in the church, because he was being reformed by the Word of God and the power of the Holy Spirit. Luther was persecuted, scorned, threatened, and charged with various kinds of frivolous misconduct by the established church. Within a few years the established church wanted Luther's life. God's wisdom and generous providence protected Luther. After Luther appeared before Charles V, the Holy Roman Emperor at the beginning of the 16th century Reformation, Luther was commanded to leave Worms and not disturb the public peace on the road home either by preaching or by writing. Luther's response was courageous.

> Before all things, humbly and from the bottom of my heart do I thank his majesty, the electors, princes, and other states of the empire, for having listened to me so kindly. I desire and have ever desired, but one thing - a reformation of the Church according to the Holy Scriptures. I am ready to do and to suffer everything in humble obedience to the emperor's will. Life or death, evil or good report - it is all the same to me, with one reservation - the preaching of the Gospel; for says St. Paul, the word of God must not be bound. (*History of Reformation*, J. H. Merle D'Aubigne, p. 252).

Luther was bound by the Word of God. Reformation was real to Luther, as any reformation is real to one whose mind, heart, and actions are bound by the Word of God.

Godly men and women love reformation. On the contrary, wicked men and women hate true reformation. They may come to a building mistakenly called the church, but they are like the opponents Paul had at Corinth, they seek to destroy the work of the gospel. Wicked men preach and teach a false gospel by peddling the Word of God. They commend themselves to the church with letters of commendation, but they seek approval by worldly methods.

Paul's letter to the Corinthians makes it clear that those wicked men who hate the gospel and therefore hate reformation are the ones who are crafty, sneaky, and they handle the Word of God deceitfully. If God's ministers (His servants) engage in the work of reformation, those who oppose reformation will disturb the work of reformation.

Godly biblical reformation is not a temporary change for the benefit of the church. Reformation according to the Word of God is founded upon an immovable permanent Rock. Any true reformation is based squarely upon the Word of God. Paul was reformed by the Word of God. Paul quoted from the book of Psalms (Psalm 116:10); "It is written: 'I believed and therefore I spoke'" (2 Corinthians 4:13).

Paul the apostle, inspired, eminent, a theological genius and a philosophical contemporary consulted the Word of God from the Old Testament for the ministry of reformation. Returning to the Scriptures and consulting the whole counsel of God is the way to reformation. Paul's ministry of reformation for the Corinthians was to bring everything into captivity to the obedience of Christ.

All ministers are instruments of reformation, and even though they have faith, knowledge, and words, they are merely instruments. Ministers who serve God, are earthen vessels (2 Corinthians 4:7). God molds them for His purpose and for His glory. Paul does not use the singular vessel, but vessels, plural, which implies that all Christians possess this characteristic. It is a great honor to be called by God to be a bearer of the gospel, because the object is supremely greater than the vessel. The man is not a treasure, but the gospel is a treasure.

The gospel finds every man in a state of spiritual poverty. Jesus said, "blessed are the poor in spirit, for theirs is the kingdom of heaven" (Matthew 5:3). The poor in spirit realize their dependence on God. Christians will find strength in weakness if they confess their spiritual poverty. "Poor in spirit" is not a financial or emotional condition. The Psalmist understood his spiritual poverty. "This poor man cried out, and the LORD heard him, and saved him out of all his troubles" (Psalm 34:6). Humility is a mark of a spiritually poor man.

> Let all those who seek You rejoice and be glad in You; Let such as love Your salvation say continually, 'The LORD be magnified!' But I am poor and needy; Yet the LORD thinks upon me. You are my help and my deliverer; Do not delay, O my God" (Psalm 40:16-17).

Pride often keeps the professing believer from realizing his or her spiritual poverty. Humility will hasten one to confess his or her spiritual poverty. The story of the prodigal son is an example of a man who realized his spiritual poverty because God humbled him (Luke 15:11-32). He realized his spiritual bankruptcy because he was poor in spirit. He was conscious of his misery and want. His pride was broken and he realized that he was helpless without the Spirit of God.

Jesus warned the church at Laodicea and by extension He warns the contemporary church of spiritual poverty. Jesus said, "you say, 'I am rich, have become wealthy, and have need of nothing'—and do not know that you are wretched, miserable, poor, blind, and naked" (Revelation 3:17). Self centeredness is the sin that prevents individual Christians and the church collectively from being "poor in spirit." Jesus was the most humble minister to ever visit the human race.

> Let this mind be in you which was also in Christ Jesus, who, being in the form of God, did not consider it robbery to be equal with God, but made Himself of no reputation, taking the form of a bondservant, and coming in the likeness of men. And being found in appearance as a man,

He humbled Himself and became obedient to the point of death, even the death of the cross. (Philippians 2:5-8)

Servants must reform themselves by removing self-confidence and replacing it with confidence in God. Break the desire for self-importance and make God important. Deny the pretense of self-righteousness and depend on the promise of God's righteousness. "For I say to you, that unless your righteousness exceeds the righteousness of the scribes and Pharisees, you will by no means enter the kingdom of heaven" (Matthew 5:20). If Christians are poor in spirit now, they will be rich in spirit when they dwell in the New Heavens and the New Earth.

Reformation is not real until Christians realize they stand before God as earthen vessels that believe the gospel and are ready to dispense it to those who will receive it. Coming to the realization that we're nothing but clay pots is major breakthrough. Most people in this day and age think of themselves as cast iron pots. Israel had the same mistaken idea just before God allowed Babylon to destroy the temple and take the covenant ministers captive.

There is a question that every minister of God ought to ask. Am I an earthen vessel? If you are an earthen vessel you are very humble, because you know you are very fragile and easily broken. If you are an earthen vessel, you must be filled in order to have value and worth. If you are an earthen vessel filled with the treasure of the gospel, then no thief can steal your treasure. Oh, you may face bumps, cracks, or breaks, but God will not deliver you over to your opponents.

True ministers of the gospel depend on the excellence of the power of God for reformation even in the face of opposition. Even So, the apostle Paul warns the church to expect opposition as we seek biblical reformation. Christians are not exempt from trouble, tribulation, and affliction. Jesus suffered more than all other men put together. Paul ministered in the face of those opposed to reformation in the church. We will meet opposition, as Charles Hodge says, "in every way and on every occasion."

We are perplexed, but not in despair. The Greek word translated "perplexed" means he is at a loss as to what to say. Apparently, Paul's crafty opponents had driven him to wonder why they could not understand the Word of God. Then Paul explains that Christians are persecuted, but not forsaken. God will never abandon his children. They may be struck down, but not destroyed. This reminds me of Job. God allowed Satan to persecute Job, but Satan did not have the power to destroy Job.

If God has called you to Himself, you have a Savior who loves you and gave Himself for you. The Lord Jesus Christ is not unaware of your suffering for the gospel. He was mistreated, defamed, oppressed and exposed to death by his opponents. We cannot be separated from Christ, so the apostle Paul says we "always carry about in the body the dying of the Lord Jesus, that the life of Jesus also may be manifested in our body" (2 Corinthians 4:10). The passion of every godly servant ought to be dying to self and living for Christ.

Ministers are reformed when they treasure the work of the Holy Spirit revealing the saving grace of Jesus Christ in the Word of God. They know Christ and love Him more each day. The Spirit and the Word will reform God's servants to resemble Jesus Christ, a treasure that is worth the race required to obtain it.

8 Reality Ministry

2 Corinthians 4:16 - 5:5

Television reality shows have become popular. They allege to focus on the reality of life based on experience. As with most postmodern entertainment, the meaning of reality is obscured. Webster's dictionary describes reality in terms of "the state of quality of being real." The Greek philosopher, Parmenides, describes reality in terms of "What is, is." Parmenides was closer to the truth of reality than postmodern reality shows.

The Word of God is profoundly real. Fascinated with reality shows, modern man ignores the reality of God and His kingdom. Unbelievers limit reality to secular sensations (sight, smell, taste, touch, sound). The Bible explains the true concept of reality. "For the things which are seen are temporary, but the things which are not seen are eternal" (2 Corinthians 4:18). Paul explains the reality ministry in his letter to the Corinthians.

The orthodox Christian concept known as reality has taken a back seat to chance, private interpretation, and individualism. To choose chance over reality is like taking a plunge over the precipice to the unknown.

Even though many people have never heard of the Heisenberg theory, it has changed the course of history. Werner Heisenberg was a Dutch physicist who changed the thinking of the scientific and philosophical world with his principle of uncertainty.

Most Christians do not understand the technicalities of his theory, but it certainly expanded the inquiry into probability thinking for the scientist and created serious fallout on the law of causality. The most dangerous effect found its way into the lives of most people in the western world, because it replaced reality with mysticism. The philosopher Stanley Jaki believes we are playing a "dangerous game" with reality. Jaki said, "Heisenberg...rejected, in the name of quantum mechanics any concern about reality as such..." (*Not a Chance*, by R. C. Sproul, p. 97). A principle in physics influenced philosophers and theologians with the notion that, in reality, God is not in control and metaphysics is merely a game. It has created the notion that reality may not be real.

Reality is real because it describes that which actually is. Reality refers to real objects, some of which may be seen and some may not be seen. After everything is said and done, ultimate reality is invisible. God and His spiritual kingdom is ultimate reality; it is eternal reality. Secular reality is temporary. It appears that Christians are more concerned with temporary appearances than they are with ultimate reality.

One reason for the lack of interest in ultimate reality is for the past few generations the church leadership has dumbed-down its church members. If Christians walk around with foggy minds, their understanding of reality will be obscure. Recent church history reveals church leaders focusing on secular management theories and psychology for the sake of growth thus ignoring solid food of the Word of God. Therefore, the poor church member continues to be fed a small indigestible portion of spiritual pabulum.

The Holy Spirit enables the Christian mind to think. I hope the Spirit of God will further enable you to think seriously about reality. Paul's letter to the Corinthians has every thing to do with reality. In fact, it has everything to do with the reality of the visible and the invisible.

The historical and grammatical context of Paul's letter is really important. Paul wrote to the Corinthian church because his opponents tried to discredit his ministry and the gospel of Christ.

Paul's ministry to the Corinthian Church was sincere and as Paul said, "we speak in the sight of God in Christ" (2 Corinthians 2:17). His opponents were apparently confessing Christians or maybe Judizers.

Their exact theological position may not be clear, but certainly Paul referred to their, "peddling the Word of God" (2 Corinthians 2:17). They were charlatans. They were quacks. They were impostors. They did not meet the standards of a true minister of the gospel, so they were not dealing with the reality of the gospel of Christ.

The apostle Paul not only dealt with the reality of the gospel, he dealt with reality in the most profound sense. Paul said, "even though our outward man is perishing, yet the inward man is being renewed day by day" (2 Corinthians 4:16). The outward man is the physical manifestation of the human being and as Paul explains, the body is in the process of being destroyed. The inward man is being renewed. The inward man is that which cannot be seen, but is very real. The inward man refers to the invisible eternal soul. The soul is invisible, but the soul expresses the reality of secular man.

The visibility of the soul is evident by the outward results. The mind is invisible, but the Christian mind understands truth. Therefore, the mind expresses itself intuitively and creatively with intelligent communication. The will motivates and compels someone to make a decision. The affections (emotions) entertain the decision and one may see the result of the decision as beautiful or ugly or lovely or detestable, and so on.

The soul is often thought of in mystical terms, yet the Bible never speaks of the soul in a mystical sense and sound reason militates against the mysticism of the soul. The soul finds its meaning in ultimate reality. There is more to life than just what meets the eye. Every servant of God, from the least of them to the greatest, must share in the reality ministry. This secular life is full of trouble, trials, and tribulation. The apostle Paul is a good example. Paul faced personal troubles most Christians will never experience. He experienced poverty and his body was weak and sometimes homeless. His enemies persecuted him with beatings, stoning, and imprisonment. Paul was once shipwrecked and constantly faced opposition by his opponents. Paul even despaired for his life.

Paul needed renewal day by day and likewise Christians today are in need of renewal day by day. The Spirit of God supplies strength without fail when it is needed to glorify God. Paul understood trouble and he understood how trouble and reality meet.

The modern world has brought a curse upon the inhabitants of its age, which appears to be getting worse rather than better. Christians in the United States have grown accustomed to comfort and luxury. Christians are so accustomed to the conveniences of this temporary world, that they give little attention to the reality of the unseen. The failure to acknowledge reality is one reason they depend on sense perception. Unfortunately many Christians have adopted the mistaken notion that image is everything.

If Christians focus only upon sense perception, they will fall into despair. It is the reality of the invisible that prevents Christians from losing heart. Cynicism is the natural course that people will follow if there is no hope for the future. I am certain of one thing; my body will terminate at some point in the future. If there is nothing beyond what I see now in this natural world, then I am the master of all cynics. The reality of what Christ did 2000 years ago when he sacrificially gave his life to save His people is the great Christian hope. The reality ministry takes Christians beyond the secular pain and misery to real life, which is eternal. The inspired Word of God says it best. "For we know that if our earthly house is destroyed, we have a building from God, a house not made with hands, eternal in the heavens" (2 Corinthians 5:1).

Paul looked forward to the unseen things because in this present visible world he groaned, desiring to enter his heavenly home. Contrast Paul's thinking to that of the majority of the western world today and you will find the secular world joining hands with chance. There is little interest in the reality of the visible or the invisible. It does not require a scientist, philosopher, or theologian to figure out that the reality of the visible is death. On the other hand, God's people are assured of the reality of the invisible and the blessed state of existence after death.

If you expect to take pleasure in the things unseen, you must understand two things. Humans cannot see the invisible things God has prepared because His invisible kingdom was not created with human hands. Mere human reason cannot possibly understand the reality of the invisible things the God has created for our good and for His glory. There is a sense of mystery in the reality of God. Paul's letter to the Colossians summarizes the reality ministry.

> For I want you to know what a great conflict I have for you and those in Laodicea, and for as many as have not seen my face in the flesh, that their hearts may be encouraged, being knit together in love, and attaining to all riches of the full assurance of understanding, to the knowledge of the mystery of God, both of the Father and of Christ, in whom are hidden all the treasures of wisdom and knowledge. (Colossians 2:1-3)

The reality ministry begins with every believer participating in the ministry. It is a ministry of unique fellowship and encouragement. "Full assurance" refers to the highest level of objective trust relative to understanding reality. "...[T]he knowledge of the mystery of God, both of the Father and of Christ, in whom are hidden all the treasures of wisdom and knowledge" is unadulterated ministry to the church. The church will have spiritual strength when God's servants feed each other the ministry of reality.

9 Life, Death, and Judgment

2 Corinthians 5:6-11

Benjamin Franklin allegedly said, "there is nothing certain in this life except death and taxes." Life and death are subjects of interminable discussion. Philosophers have occupied their time with understanding life and inquiring into death.

The epitaph etched on a grave marker: "That he, who many a year, with toil of breath, found death in life, may here find life in death." One Greek philosopher said, "Perhaps death is life, and life is death. For what is death but an eternal sleep? And does not life consist in sleeping and eating."

Life is an interesting phenomenon. I say phenomenon because most people only think of life in terms of the senses. The definition of life might escape many of us because more often than not our definition of life is the opposite of death. Then we ask: what is death? Death is a subject that we not only don't understand, but too often we avoid the subject. Yet the Bible uses the words die or death hundreds of times. Sometimes it refers to the termination of this bodily life. Other times it speaks of the death of the soul. However, the death of the soul does not literally refer to the termination of the soul.

The Bible speaks of life in several different ways.

1) literal – "all the days of your life" (Genesis 3:14)
2) figurative – "the tree of life" (Genesis 2:9)
3) eternal life – "that you may have eternal life" (1 John 5:13)

The Christian should have a radically different view of life and death than the unbeliever.

9 Life, Death, and Judgment

The Christian should understand the reality of this visible world is a gift of God. They should appreciate that gift and act as good stewards over the life God has given. However, Christians should understand the reality of the invisible. Although we cannot see the unseen things God has in store for us, we should appreciate them and live with a joyous expectation of receiving them.

Paul had a clear understanding of life and death. Life is one "whether present or absent" from this body. The emphasis in today's world is on the physical body and the experience people often call life. While Christians are in this body their emphasis should be on stewardship. Their time in this body should be a time of service and good stewardship as well as a time of preparation for their eternal estate in the New Heavens and the New Earth.

Christians have only one life, but they have two homes. One home is in the present physical body and the other home is eternal in the New Heavens and the New Earth.

The apostle says, "we are always confident" which indicates a certain boldness about the life not yet seen. Christians should be confident that God will supply a New body fit for eternal wear and tear. There is a sense in which our present body is not a very good home. The infirmities of the body make it an inconvenient place to live. It is weak, fickle, capricious, and subject to destruction.

Jesus reminded his disciples of a truth that fits well with this text on life. Jesus said, "The thief comes only to steal and kill, and destroy; I came that they might have life and might have it abundantly" (John 10:10). Our present bodies are subject to death and destruction and that is the reason we need the abundance of God's grace for life. The abundance of God's grace gives life that will continue until the Lord gives us a permanent eternal body. Our confidence is not in some esoteric existential experience that promises a place called heaven. Christians must have a sound rational understanding of the resurrection. That is our confidence.

Furthermore, as Christians, our confidence is not in our mortal being. The apostle Paul wanted his mortality to be swallowed up by life (2 Corinthians 5:4). He did not desire death, but he did expect the resurrection of the body to remove all corruption, weakness, and death. These are not just passing thoughts. They belong to the Christian world and life view. Our confidence in the reality of life with God is as sure as anything we know and believe.

If our hope and confidence is real, that confidence should not be a temporary passing fad based on some religious experience. The life of the soul finds its meaning in ultimate reality. It is ultimate reality that provides a right perspective on life. It is also ultimate reality that provides a clear understanding of death.

Once Christians grasp the meaning of ultimate reality and how it brings into focus life and death, then they can be ambitious to please the Lord in all things. Man ought to live to finish what God expects of him. Then he should be ready to die for the glory of God.

Does life and death provoke Christians to think about their relationship with God? Do they endeavor to demonstrate Christly character in their day to day activities? Is their great ambition in life to please the Lord? Christians should take those questions very serious. If they believe the Bible they will surely find themselves contemplating and meditating over those questions, because they know there is a day of accountability.

Judgment is as certain as death and the Bible asserts that everyone will appear before the judgment seat of Christ. The judgment seat is not a very good place according to my understanding of the judgment seat from the rest of Scripture. Pilate was said to have sat on the judgment seat when he heard from Christ (John 19:13). Then the apostle Paul refers to the judgment seat in his letter to the Romans and his letter to the

Corinthians. For some strange reason, many Christians do not think they will have to stand before the eternal Judge. They say once you become a Christian, there is no more judgment. The evidence in Scripture is powerfully persuasive that Christians will stand before the all-powerful divine Judge of heaven and earth.

> "God will judge the secrets of men through Christ Jesus." (Romans 2:16)
> "The Lord will judge His people." (Hebrews 10:30)
>
> "It is appointed for men to die once and after this comes judgment." (Hebrews 9:27)
>
> "And I saw the dead the great and the small, standing before the throne, and books were opened; and another book was opened, which is the book of life; and the dead were judged from the things which were written in the books, according to their deeds." (Revelation 20:12)

One of the events in the final judgment is that "the book of life will be opened." The text in Revelation is smothered in symbolism, but there is one certainty, the book of life is an absolute standard. It is not a matter of someone's opinion. The pure truth will be revealed from this book.

First, the book of life tests the legal standing with God. Then it measures the moral constitution of the soul, not as man sees it, but as God sees it. At the judgment seat, there are no private meetings, no special preferences. That which was private in this life will become public.

> All grudges will be opened for all to see.
> All gossip will be exposed as lies.
> All slander will be vindicated publicly.

If Christians believe the Bible, they must believe in the judgment seat of Christ. If they believe there will be a judgment seat for all men, then it should affect their understanding of life and death.

Another positive effect of the judgment seat of Christ; it is the place God's children are given rewards for doing good. I cannot stress enough that although Christians will stand before the judgment seat, they will not find condemnation or eternal punishment. The Christian is forgiven, his works are tested, and he is given his rewards according to his works. The Bible does not give the specific details about the rewards, because if we are indeed Christians, we seek not the high place, but rather we seek the faithful place. This will be a righteous judgment, because Jesus Christ is a righteous judge. The righteous Judge is a loving Savior to all who will believe.

Christians will never understand the final judgment until they understand the biblical doctrine of forgiveness. The Word of God is manifest in its doctrine of forgiveness.

> "If we confess our sins, He is faithful and just to forgive us our sins and to cleanse us from all unrighteousness" (1 John 1:9).

> "For if you forgive men their trespasses, your heavenly Father will also forgive you. But if you do not forgive men their trespasses, neither will your Father forgive your trespasses" Matthew 6:14-15).

The guilt of inherited sin and actual sins must be confessed to God and He will forgive. Likewise you have to forgive brothers and sisters in Christ. The Word of God prescribes the perfect (inspired) doctrine of forgiveness for Christians.

> Moreover if your brother sins against you, go and tell him his fault between you and him alone. If he hears you, you have gained your brother. But if he will not hear, take with you one or two more, that 'by the mouth of two or three witnesses every word may be established.' And if he refuses to hear them, tell it to the church. But if he refuses even to hear the church, let him be to you like a heathen and a tax collector. Assuredly, I say to you, whatever you bind on earth will be bound in heaven, and whatever you loose on earth will be loosed in heaven. (Mathew 18:15-18)

Forgiveness is so important the Bible covers it from every perspective.

> Therefore if you bring your gift to the altar, and there remember that your brother has something against you, leave your gift there before the altar, and go your way. First be reconciled to your brother, and then come and offer your gift. Agree with your adversary quickly, while you are on the way with him, lest your adversary deliver you to the judge, the judge hand you over to the officer, and you be thrown into prison. Assuredly, I say to you, you will by no means get out of there till you have paid the last penny.(Matthew 5:23-26)

Forgiveness must come from the heart. "So My heavenly Father also will do to you if each of you, from his heart, does not forgive his brother his trespasses" (Matthew 18:35).

Forgiveness must include full forgiveness. "As far as the east is from the west, so far has He removed our transgressions from us" (Psalm 103:12).

God's attitude toward forgiveness uniquely belongs to Him, but God has revealed several aspects of forgiveness. The transcendence of God does not allow us to see the full objective nature of His forgiveness. Scripture, however, teaches that a number of factors may affect divine forgiveness.

> a. Weakness
> "as far as the east is from the west, so far has he removed our transgressions from us...for he knows how we are formed, he remembers that we are dust" (Psalm 103:12-14).
>
> b. Ignorance
> "Jesus said, 'Father forgive them, for they do not know what they are doing'" (Luke 23:34).
>
> c. The presence of righteous men in a sinful society: "Go up and down the streets of Jerusalem, look around and consider, search through her squares. If you can find but one person who deals honestly and seeks the truth, I will forgive this city" (NIV, Jeremiah 5:1).

The unbeliever stands condemned in the judgment. The believer rejoices in the judgment. The revelation from Scripture is that Jesus Christ will judge the human race. I pray that the Word of God and the power of His Spirit will enable and enlighten your understanding of life, death, and judgment.

10 Reunion Ministry

2 Corinthians 5:12-21

The Christian church is an important part of life in this country. Without the church providing a biblical ethic, morality would be a matter of personal preference. Chaos would result except for general revelation and natural law. Without the church metaphysics would be a personal relative opinion of the things that exist apart from this present world. The ministry of the church goes beyond the scope of this world. The Christian church is a ministry. It teaches morality and provides an academic platform for metaphysical inquiry. More importantly, the church is the place to hear the message of salvation.

Paul's letter to the Corinthians infers that the ministry of the apostle was the target of criticism by some of the church members at Corinth. Paul's opponents tried to discredit him, but Paul made it clear that he conducted himself "in simplicity and godly sincerity, not with fleshly wisdom" (2 Corinthians 1:12). Contrary to the charges against him, the inspired apostle makes it clear that his opponents "walk in craftiness and handle the Word of God deceitfully."

Even with all the trouble at Corinth, it was still a local Christian church. Another picture of the true church is found in the book of Revelation. The Lord said, "the seven lampstands which you saw are the seven churches" (Revelation 1:20). John's reference to the lampstands comes from the Old Testament. The lampstand in the temple held the oil that provided light. If the lampstand had no oil, there was no light. The picture in the book of Revelation is the true church shines as the oil of the Spirit is burning thus making the church a light on the hill.

Every individual Christian and every individual church must ask the question: "Is the Spirit of the Lord burning in my life and in the church family?" Before responding with a hasty answer, consider the full counsel of God.

God's Word speaks to that question. "He flatters himself in his own eyes, when he finds out his iniquity and when he hates" (Psalm 36:2). Anyone who flatters himself or herself should check to see if the oil of the Spirit is burning in the soul. The New International Version has an easy to understand translation. "He flatters himself too much to detect or hate his sin."

Paul may have that Psalm in mind when he wrote the Corinthians and referred to "those who boast in appearance and not in heart" (2 Corinthians 5:12). The unconverted sinner amuses himself with various ideas, thinking that he might dismiss the coming judgment of God. So they put on a front. Image is everything and substance is zero. The idea is that his heart is so hardened that he applauds his own sin. So where does this leave the ministry of the church?

If an unbeliever remains outside the church, his boasting and flattery is to his own disgrace. However, if a church member "boasts in appearance and not in heart" his boasting and flattery is to the disgrace of the church. When a church member flatters himself too much to detect or hate his sin you can be sure that the ministry of the church will suffer.

The sin in the church today is the same as it was at Corinth. The strife, bickering, and contention enlarge; therefore, the ministry suffers. Paul speaks plain to the Corinthian church, so that all future Corinthian churches will have the benefit of his inspired words.

The conflict that causes alienation and division is the sin and corruption inherited from Adam. The *Westminster Confession of Faith* explains this doctrine. "By this sin they fell from their original righteousness and communion with God and so became dead in sin and wholly defiled in all the faculties and parts of soul and body" (*Westminster Confession of Faith*, 6.1).

The depraved state of sinful humanity renders individuals spiritually dead, incapable, and unworthy. They were "alienated" from God. This alienation was the result of spiritual rebellion and contumacy, not a lack of academic knowledge or religious failure.

This barrier of sin is truly a problem in man's relationship to God. Scripture leaves no doubt as to the corruption of mankind and the fact that this corruption, which is an effrontery before God, required reconciliation. Reunion is necessary because there was once a union between God and man that was unique in every sense of the word. There is a principle involved that profoundly affects the ministry of the Christian church. "Behold, I was brought forth in iniquity, And in sin my mother conceived me" (Psalm 51:5). All human beings come into the world disaffected from God. The principle carries over to human relationships. Sin drives a wedge between friends and the doctrine of forgiveness brings the celebration of a reunion. The book of Romans explains the ministry of reunion.

> Much more then, having now been justified by His blood, we shall be saved from wrath through Him. For if when we were enemies we were reconciled to God through the death of His Son, much more, having been reconciled, we shall be saved by His life. And not only that, but we also rejoice in God through our Lord Jesus Christ, through whom we have now received the reconciliation. (Romans 5:9-11)

This text mentions justification and reconciliation and the two are similar relative to salvation.

> Verse 9 - much more by His blood we shall be saved
> Verse 10 - much more through the death of His Son we shall be saved

However there are some differences relative to the ministry Christ provides for God's people.

Verse 9 - having now been justified by His blood
Verse 10 - we were reconciled to God through the death of His Son

Justification and reconciliation are necessary for salvation.

Verse 9 - we shall be saved from wrath through Him
Verse 10 - we shall be saved by His life

Christians are justified by the blood of Christ and reconciled through the death of God's Son. Blood is important because the believer's standing before God is the result of the Blood of Christ not philosophical truth or moral influence. The death of Christ is important because it is necessary to satisfy God's wrath.

Justification is legal language. As a metaphor, justification is similar to a courtroom scene. It is the picture of a guilty criminal, declared innocent by the judge. Reconciliation describes the bringing together of two parties. Reconciliation describes the restoration of broken relationships.

For instance, two nations at war sign a peace treaty and they are reconciled. Two individuals at enmity with each other ask forgiveness, thus they are reconciled. From birth, unconverted sinful man is at war with God. The only hope is that God will declare the man "not guilty" and change the relationship so peace will be the result.

The grace of justification finds its ultimate joy in the grace of reconciliation. In the case of man being reconciled with God, the reconciliation was possible because of the ministry of Jesus Christ. He not only brought reconciliation and an end to enmity between God and sinners, but it also is the means of reconciliation between individuals.

> For He Himself is our peace, who has made both one, and has broken down the middle wall of separation, having abolished in His flesh the enmity, that is, the law of commandments contained in ordinances, so as to create in Himself one New man from the two, thus making peace, and that He might reconcile them both to God in one body through the cross, thereby putting to death the enmity. And He came and preached peace to you who were afar off and to those who were near. (Ephesians 2:14-17)

What God has done through the Lord Jesus Christ will change the lives of people and those people will assemble as God's people in peace and harmony. There are several different noticeable changes after God reconciles sinners to Himself. First, they became New creatures; old things passed away. The converted sinner becomes a new creation in Christ. He or she adopts a new world and life view. The ministry of reconciliation between God and man should get the attention of a shattered church.

Reconciliation according to the Bible is not just mutual reconciliation, but an act of God forgiving those former sins and not even looking upon them. When God reconciles His people to Himself it is evidence of His forgiveness. Unforgiven sin is deadly. Unforgiven sin is waiting to erupt like an active volcano.

Another noticeable change comes when God reconciles sinners to Himself. "They are not only given the ministry of reconciliation" (2 Corinthians 5:18), which marks the change in their soul and life, but God commits to them the "word of reconciliation" (2 Corinthians 5:19). If you are one of God's children, then you are a minister in the church, and if you are a minister in the church, then God has given you the ministry of reconciliation by His word and Spirit.

The word of reconciliation is the word of reunion with God, by faith in Jesus Christ alone, by the power of the Holy Spirit alone. When God reconciles sinners to Himself, it is the duty of the converted sinner to be reconciled with those whom God has called to Himself. The apostle John presents a picture that confirms Paul's doctrine of reconciliation. "If someone says, I love God, and hates his brother, he is a liar; for he who does not love his brother whom he has seen, how can he love God whom he has not seen" (1 John 4:21). The practice of reconciliation is the evidence for the ministry of reunion in the church.

In John's letter, in Matthew's gospel, in Paul's letter to the Corinthians, and in many other places, the Bible presents the doctrine of reconciliation in clear and compelling terms. If you are a child of God, then you are an ambassador of Christ, as Paul says, and you have the awesome responsibility to plead with all men to be reconciled to God.

11 Ministry After Reconciliation

2 Corinthians 6:1-10

Paul's ministry to the Corinthian Church was to turn it into a ministering church. The biblical minister is one who serves in the church of our Lord Jesus Christ. It is a great privilege to serve in the church. Jesus Christ is head of the church, the Lord and giver of life. His disciples are servants who are the recipients of life. Christians are not merely obligated to serve God, they are compelled to serve Him as their Master. Any servant who loves his master will serve the master. The church has ignored the servant/master concept which means she has forgotten the minister/ministry concept.

Christian ministers are new creatures in Christ because Christ has reconciled them to Himself so they might have the ministry of reconciliation. Christians must come to this text with the mind and heart of one who has been reconciled to God and man, so they cannot but want to serve God and man according to the ministry God gives them. Ministry after reconciliation should be the delight of every Christian.

The first and highest ministry of a minister is to serve God by worshipping Him, in private and in public. Paul commended the Thessalonians as they turned to God from idols to serve a living and true God (1 Thessalonians 1:9). After unbelieving sinners are reconciled to God, they will have a passionate desire to worship God according to His word.

God's displeasure towards false worship does not have a good ending. Christians ought to read the account of false worship in Leviticus chapter ten. The Lord gave specific instructions for offering worship relative to the use of fire and incense (Leviticus 16:12). It is clear that God commanded them to worship a specific way and they offered worship "which He had not commanded them" (Leviticus 10:1-2). Nabad and Abihu were punished most severely for their disobedience in worship.

Generational continuity is necessary to pass along the doctrine, form, and expression of true worship. Failure to teach each generation the principles of godly and true worship will give rise to the ugly faces of false worship.

Eli's sons sinned in the context of worship. Apparently Eli failed to correct them and teach them the proper way to worship God. Furthermore they did not know the Lord (1 Samuel 2:12). Eli should not have allowed them to lead in worship. Eli's failure provoked "the Lord to judge his house forever for the iniquity which he knew, because his sons brought a curse on themselves and he did not rebuke them (1 Samuel 3:13). (*Joy in Worship*, by James Vickery, p. 22-23).

The reason Christians worship God the way He commands them to worship Him here and now, is so they will be ready to worship Him in their eternal home. The Bible speaks of service and worship to God in the New Heavens and New Earth in the slave/master relationship. "And there shall be no more curse, but the throne of God and of the Lamb shall be in it, and His servants shall serve Him" (Revelation 22:3). It is indisputable that one could be reconciled to God and have no desire to worship and serve God.

God reconciles His children to Himself so they will be enabled to reconcile with each other. Another indisputable truth in Scripture is that God's people minister to each other after they are reconciled to each other. Paul's letter to the church at Rome reveals ministry to one another.

> But now I am going to Jerusalem to minister to the saints. For it pleased those from Macedonia and Achaia to make a certain contribution for the poor among the saints who

are in Jerusalem. It pleased them indeed, and they are their debtors. For if the Gentiles have been partakers of their spiritual things, their duty is also to minister to them in material things. (Romans 15:25-27)

As Christians minister to each other's needs, they must remember that they are not sinless people. Christian ministry requires people to interact and relate to each other. Christian ministers find themselves vulnerable to all sorts of criticism, even as they try to minister to the needs of others.

Paul said, "We give no offense in anything, that our ministry may not be blamed" (2 Corinthians 6:3). The *New American Standard Bible* translation clarifies this text in agreement with the Greek text translating it, "give no cause for offense." Paul warns Christians to be careful not to be a cause for offense, so that their ministry will not receive criticism. Paul does not mean that Christians might be perceived as offensive, but they should aspire to remain guiltless as to the cause of offense. Paul was not successful in avoiding a perceived offense. Even the gospel was considered offensive by some.

Corinth like many other churches was too quick to let personalities enter into consideration. They should have thought in terms of the gospel and the truth from Scripture. The only way to stand against false accusations or misplaced perceived offenses is to be faithful as a minister of God according to the Word of God.

Paul's comment to the Corinthians appears to have subtle irony in the message. "We commend ourselves as ministers of God" (2 Corinthians 6:4). The irony is that Christians are supposed to be on the offensive without being the cause for offense. The way to accomplish that is for Christians to demonstrate that they are ministers of God. Ministers do not commend themselves for self-vindication, yet the credibility of the messenger and the message is important to the advancement of the gospel.

Christians must not attempt to commend themselves by self-praise, self-aggrandizement, false ambition, handling the Word of God deceitfully, or walking in craftiness. If they expect to minister effectively as servants of God, they must be careful in both doctrine and practice. If their preaching, teaching, and evangelizing is built on false doctrine, then the ministry is dead before it gets started.

The Word of God is God's objective standard for ministry. The Word of God is very specific about the circumstances and challenges a minister may face. In the course of God's providence many things happen that seem to militate or go against the purpose of our call as ministers. How should we respond to the circumstances occurring in the providence of God? Ministers (all God's servants) must endure the trials that come their way.

Paul listed the trials that came his way. Although Christians may not face the same identical circumstances, they must be prepared to trust God and face the trials that come their way. Paul faced general trials such as tribulations, needs, and distresses. It should not surprise Christians when they, as ministers of Christ's church, meet trouble and hardships for the sake of Christ. Paul also faced specific trials that he called stripes, imprisonments, and tumults.

In America those trials are almost unheard of, yet in many countries of the world Christians are often beaten, imprisoned or face some kind of physical punishment just because they speak the gospel to someone. Christians should not entertain the idea that just because they have unique religious freedom that they are free of any trials.

Paul subjected himself to trials for the sake of his ministry. He said he was a minister in labors, in sleeplessness, and in fastings. There is nothing wrong with a little hard work, a few nights without sleep, and doing without a meal so Christians might commend themselves as ministers of God to the world which needs the gospel ministry.

Ministers of the church of Jesus Christ must also have a reputation that fits the ministry. Ministers should be known for their purity, knowledge, longsuffering, and kindness. Ministers must have a desire for holiness of life. Ministers must have a knowledge of God, the gospel and the ministry to which they have been called.

Ministers cannot commend themselves as ministers unless they patiently submit to the injustice and personal attacks by the workers of iniquity. They cannot commend themselves as ministers unless they have a disposition to do good and be useful in the ministry to which God has called them.

The best part of ministry after reconciliation is that God gives His children the resources to be effective ministers. If you feel inadequate to minister you should take a good look at your resources. Pray for the Holy Spirit to fill your soul with sincere love and the Word of God. You must have the Holy Spirit to be a minister for Jesus Christ. You must demonstrate sincere love for God, His people and the whole world. Truth is the only possible weapon that will give you a successful ministry against Satan.

If God has reconciled you to Himself and equipped you for ministry in the church you will be able to face all distresses. You are called to serve God as his minister. God saves His people to serve. In this world of self interest, self love, and self service, God's people are called to minister after reconciliation.

12 Complex Ministry

2 Corinthians 6:11-7:1

Christians believe the Word of God is unique in every sense of the word. Unfortunately, too many conservative evangelicals and fundamentalists have come to worship the Word of God rather than the God of the Word.

When you read or hear the Word of God, what kind of imagery, if any, comes to your mind? Does the text in Paul's letter to the Corinthians bring to your mind a picture of his concern for the Christians at Corinth and by extension his concern for the whole church?

Paul has been defending his ministry to the Corinthians against the attacks of false teachers who came to Corinth to oppose Paul's ministry. They apparently tried, unsuccessfully, to discredit Paul and his ministry. For those at Corinth who may be tempted to follow the false teachers, Paul has this message: " Be reconciled and carry the ministry of reconciliation with you to your family and neighbors."

Did Paul expect the Corinthian Christians to be reconciled with those false teachers? Paul may have desired reconciliation with those false teachers, but let's face it, they may not have been Christians. They may profess to be Christians, but in reality they may not be Christians.

The parable of the wheat and tares will help God's children understand the Corinthian dilemma.

> Another parable He put forth to them, saying: "The kingdom of heaven is like a man who sowed good seed in his field; but while men slept, his enemy came and sowed tares among the wheat and went his way. But when the grain had sprouted and produced a crop, then the tares also appeared. So the servants of the owner came and said

> to him, 'Sir, did you not sow good seed in your field? How then does it have tares?' He said to them, 'An enemy has done this.' The servants said to him, 'Do you want us then to go and gather them up?' But he said, 'No, lest while you gather up the tares you also uproot the wheat with them. Let both grow together until the harvest, and at the time of harvest I will say to the reapers, "First gather together the tares and bind them in bundles to burn them, but gather the wheat into my barn." (Matthew 13:24-30)

Then Jesus explained the meaning of the parable.

> Then Jesus sent the multitude away and went into the house. And His disciples came to Him, saying, "Explain to us the parable of the tares of the field." He answered and said to them: "He who sows the good seed is the Son of Man. The field is the world, the good seeds are the sons of the kingdom, but the tares are the sons of the wicked one. The enemy who sowed them is the devil, the harvest is the end of the age, and the reapers are the angels. Therefore as the tares are gathered and burned in the fire, so it will be at the end of this age. The Son of Man will send out His angels, and they will gather out of His kingdom all things that offend, and those who practice lawlessness, and will cast them into the furnace of fire. There will be wailing and gnashing of teeth. Then the righteous will shine forth as the sun in the kingdom of their Father. He who has ears to hear, let him hear! (Matthew 13:36-43)

The enemy in this parable is a vicious unrelenting demonic person. The tares were weeds and they not only destroyed the crop, but produced a fungus that was poisonous when eaten. Why would one want to destroy the work of another for no reason at all? All the labor and money invested in the field was destroyed for evil purposes.

However, the sower of tares works in darkness. He is a coward and afraid to deal with the light and reality. He does his wicked work, but he will be judged and given his due punishment. Nobody mocks God and gets away with it. Paul was not ignorant of Jesus' parable.

False teachers and unbelievers may co-exist under co-belligerent conditions, but Christians should ever keep in mind that unbelievers are not reconciled to God and therefore cannot be reconciled with men. Christians must be judicious in their dealings with all men, but with fellow Christians they must demonstrate their love for them with innermost feelings. "O Corinthians! We have spoken openly to you, our heart is wide open" (2 Corinthians 6:11). Paul loved the people of God at Corinth. Paul loved the Corinthian Christians because he loved God and he loved God because he is in a right relationship with God. It is called reconciliation.

The kind of relationship Paul had with the Christians at Corinth is almost unheard of today. Paul was open, honest, sincere and had the spiritual welfare of the Corinthian Christians in mind at all times. It was for those reasons that Paul could present the truth in love to the Corinthian Christians. Truth is necessary for any intelligent thinking. It requires intelligent thinking to understand the commandment to love one another.

The truth in love does not cause any confusion of words and doctrine found in the Word of God. Without truth in love the teaching of Scripture becomes personal relative. To put it another way, private interpretation prevails and ultimately, Scripture becomes worthless. If compromise and reconciliation are not properly interpreted, there is no biblical truth.

When Paul said Jesus Christ "has given us the ministry of reconciliation" he does not mean that we must sacrifice God's word for the sake of unity. A compromise is an arbitrary consent to mutual concessions for the sake of unity. Christians can compromise on some things and other things they cannot compromise.

> They cannot compromise the law of God.
> They cannot compromise the gospel.
> They cannot compromise any clear teaching in Scripture.

Christians can compromise on matters indifferent. They may compromise on where to meet for worship. Unfortunately, many Christians will not compromise on things indifferent, but they will compromise on the teaching of Scripture. The confusion among Christians is "how far or how much may I compromise."

Another confusing concept is reconciliation. What does the word reconciliation mean? Once there was a union among two parties, then a separation occurred. Reconciliation describes two disaffected parties re-joined together.

The confusion really multiplies when reconciliation meets compromise. For some strange reason it is widely held that Christians should not make distinctions and should constrain themselves from any righteous judgment. That is not the teaching of Scripture. Christians must not compromise the Word of God, especially on anti-Christian matters. "Do not be unequally yoked together with unbelievers." You may ask, "where did Paul find Scripture that teaches that kind of principle?" It is found in the book of Deuteronomy.

> When the LORD your God brings you into the land which you go to possess, and has cast out many nations before you, the Hittites and the Girgashites and the Amorites and the Canaanites and the Perizzites and the Hivites and the Jebusites, seven nations greater and mightier than you, and when the LORD your God delivers them over to you, you shall conquer them and utterly destroy them. You shall make no covenant with them nor show mercy to them. Nor shall you make marriages with them. You shall

not give your daughter to their son, nor take their daughter for your son. For they will turn your sons away from following Me, to serve other gods; so the anger of the LORD will be aroused against you and destroy you suddenly. But thus you shall deal with them: you shall destroy their altars, and break down their sacred pillars, and cut down their wooden images, and burn their carved images with fire. For you are a holy people to the LORD your God; the LORD your God has chosen you to be a people for Himself, a special treasure above all the peoples on the face of the earth. (Deuteronomy 7:1-6)

Other theologians believe that Paul has the Deuteronomical imperative in mind. "You shall not plow with an ox and a donkey together" (Deuteronomy 22:10). John Calvin's comment on that text was "the integrity of nature is corrupted" when animals are unnaturally joined together. For instance, the ox could pull more than the donkey. God created one species to do one thing and another species to do a different thing.

Paul's fundamental message to the church is that Christians should not enter into a covenant relationship with an unbeliever if that relationship requires you to go against the clear teaching of Scripture. Do not take a job with an unbeliever if the unbeliever requires you to cheat and defraud the customer.

Although Christians live among unbelievers and can readily converse and interact with them in many ways, there are some limitations. Paul's warnings are self-explanatory:

1) What fellowship has righteousness with lawlessness?
2) What communion has light with darkness?
3) What accord has Christ with Belial?
4) What part has a believer with an unbeliever?
5) What agreement has the temple of God with idols?

12 Complex Ministry

There is a great divide between Christian doctrine and anti-Christian doctrine. There is a great divide between Christian morals and anti-Christian morals. Christians may live among unbelievers like the wheat grows along side the tares, but they must not live like unbelievers.

The Lord our God lovingly says to his children: "I will be a Father to you, and you shall be My sons and daughters" (2 Corinthians 6:18). God's children are His ministers and their duty is to serve God. Living in a sinful world and serving a holy God may seem like a complex ministry. Therefore God's children ought to remember Paul's admonition. "Therefore having these promises, beloved, let us cleanse ourselves from all filthiness of the flesh and spirit, perfecting holiness in the fear of God" (2 Corinthians 7:1). The instruction does not refer to perfectionism, but instructs Christians to strive as ministers to please the Father in all things.

13 Minister to One Another

2 Corinthians 7:2-16

Ministry is the outworking of brotherly love. Paul demonstrated as much in his letter to the Corinthian Church. Paul expressed his feelings for the Corinthians with sincere affections. "O Corinthians! We have spoken openly to you, our heart is wide open" (2 Corinthians 6:11). The Greek grammar is enlightening because it indicates Paul's attitude toward the Corinthians. Later Paul put it in very tender language saying "you are in our hearts" (2 Corinthians 7:3). Paul expected the Corinthians to reciprocate. Paul literally commanded the Corinthians to "Open your hearts to us" (2 Corinthians 7:2).

Brotherly love encourages unity in the church. However, unity requires some agreement and assent to a body of truth. Mutual understanding is necessary, but Christian unity does not depend on absolute like-mindedness. Christians must cherish and encourage each other in truth, but as sinners they have to be careful with their claims for truth.

Individual Christians and the church collectively must not become doctrinally arrogant because, "All synods and councils since the apostles' times, whether general or particular, may err, and many have erred; therefore they are not to be made the rule of faith or practice, but to be used as an help in both" (*Westminster Confession of Faith*, 31.4). One distinction between the true church and a religious cult is that a true church never professes to have the only and complete body of religious truth, but a cult believes itself to hold the absolute and final truth on all religious matters.

Paul's insistence upon intimacy is predicated upon the Corinthians understanding of the Word of God, even though Paul did not think the Corinthians understood the Word of God as clearly as they should.

Paul said, "open your hearts to us" to enlarge their understanding of their ministry to one another. The word "heart" is not in the Greek manuscripts. However, the context demands the use of the word heart. The full description of human existence is found in the word "heart." Paul is not just talking about emotions. Paul's use of the word heart refers to how Christians think and act rationally, not just sensations, impressions or sentiments. Christians are particularly identified by intellectual and moral qualities as well as affectionate and emotional expressions. Christians open their hearts to each other for the sake of ministry. To put it another way, Christians minister to one another with their whole being. Christians must minister to each other with their minds, thinking through logical propositions and ethical values with the mind of Christ. Christian's minister to each other with their actions soundly based on God's will. Christians minister to each other affectionately. The Word of God commands Christians to open their hearts to each other, so they may minister to each other.

An open heart necessarily requires self-examination. Paul's self-examination focused on the second table of the Law. He said, "We have wronged no one, we have corrupted no one, we have cheated no one" (2 Corinthians 7:2). A closer look at these three assertions will help Christians open their eyes, so they may open their heart.

Paul's assertion was that he had not wronged anyone and committed no injustice and no physical harm against anyone. The full counsel of God reveals that Paul had acted unjustly towards Christians before his conversion. The full counsel of God also reveals that Paul had repented and was reconciled to them. The immediate context indicates Paul's relationship with the Corinthians specifically and the church at large. Every Christian ought to ask the question, "Have I wronged anyone?" The covenant people of God in the Old Testament were guilty of acting unjustly against one another. Scripture declares that they oppressed "the poor" and crushed "the needy" (Amos 4:1; Micah

2:1). Christians ought to examine the second table of the Ten Commandments before saying, "I have wronged no one. The tenth commandment commands Christians not to covet. Coveting is acting unjustly.

> Covetousness is an inclination that stands ready to motivate murder, engage in immoral sex, steal and join the company of liars. If someone desires the reputation of another man and incapable of having a good reputation, then one person slanders the other to raise his or her own ego. All because they covet something they do not have. Greed is often the cause of sexual sins. People steal because the heart covets the things of this world. Some people will not discipline themselves to think intelligently, so they tell lies to try and impress people, because they covet attention. (*Brief Study of the Ten Commandments*, by Martin Murphy, p. 104)

Christians ought to ask the question, "have I corrupted anyone"? The word "corrupted" in this text is also used in 2 Corinthians 11:3 which helps understand Paul's use of the word. "But I fear, lest somehow, as the serpent deceived Eve by his craftiness, so your minds may be corrupted from the simplicity that is in Christ. For if he who comes preaches another Jesus whom we have not preached" (2 Corinthians 11:3-4). Preaching or teaching false doctrine will corrupt the mind.

> For false christs and false prophets will rise and show great signs and wonders to deceive, if possible, even the elect. See, I have told you beforehand" (Matthew 24:24-25).

Paul also told the Corinthian Church, "we have cheated no one" or to put it another way, "Paul had not defrauded anyone." Paul's opponents may have been charging Paul with being a charlatan trying to take advantage of the people. Paul said just the opposite was the case; he had already answered the charge. "For we are not, as so many, peddling the word of God; but as of sincerity, but as from God, we speak in the sight of God in Christ" (2 Corinthians 2:17).

The same Lord Jesus Christ that saved Paul is the same Lord Jesus Christ that saved the Corinthians, so the same God must be in their hearts. If God is in their hearts, then Satan could not be there too. Paul simply looked at his heart and there God was. Paul wanted the Christians to look at their heart to see if God was there. If Christians wrong, corrupt, or cheat one another then repentance and reconciliation is necessary and certainly necessary if they expect to minister to one another in the church.

Paul's open heart request is to those who have been reconciled. They were reconciled because they had repented (2 Corinthians 7:8-10). Apparently Paul wrote them a rather strong letter that brought the sin in the church to their attention. The letter brought sorrow and according to Paul the sorrow led to repentance.

The first step toward reconciliation is repentance. The *Westminster Shorter Catechism* describes repentance.

> A saving grace, whereby a sinner out of a true sense of his sin, and apprehension of the mercy of God in Christ, doth with grief and hatred of his sin, turn from it unto God, with full purpose of, and endeavor after, new obedience" (*Westminster Shorter Catechism*, 86).

Repentance first requires a change of mind, then a change of actions. Sorrow in a godly manner is a sign of true repentance. Christians cannot expect to minister to one another unless they repent of their sins and be reconciled according to the powerful work of the Holy Spirit. The Corinthian church repented and the result of repentance led to reconciliation.

Repentance motivated diligence. The Greek word *spoude* translated "diligence" refers to the means that one uses to hasten oneself or move quickly in some given situation. Repentance that leads to reconciliation will be followed by the desire to act quickly to repair any sinful breach and restore a broken relationship.

The Corinthian Christians acted quickly to show their disapproval of sin. Their repentance produced indignation. Where they had entertained evil before, now they hated evil. Their repentance produced fear. They respected the object of their affection and love. Their repentance produced vehement desire. The Corinthians were now eager to be ministers and serve each other in the church.

Before repentance and reconciliation Christians have no real desire to serve, but after repentance and reconciliation they are driven by godly zeal and passion to serve as ministers of the gospel. Finally the apostle says "what vindication repentance produced" (2 Corinthians 7:11).

The Greek word *apologia* translated "vindication" requires some clarification. The root of the word refers to "a spoken defense." The Corinthian Christians were ready to defend the truth of the full counsel of God.

14 Liberal Ministry Needed

2 Corinthians 8:1-7

The ministry of every Christian in the church includes various responsibilities as God's covenant people. Everything Christians do in this secular life is the natural course to prepare for the eternal estate.

The secular refers to the present time, the here and now. The eternal refers to anything beyond this present world. Unfortunately, the secular is infected with sin. When sin raises its ugly head, as it did in Corinth, the ministry of the church suffers. From the secular perspective, Paul's ministry had come under attack by some false teachers, but Paul kept his head straight and confronted those in Corinth who stood in opposition to Paul. Those in the church who opposed Paul were professing Christians, so Paul had an interest in their eternal estate. It was necessary for Paul to defend his ministry or risk the possibility that the false teachers would deceive the whole church with their crafty cunning lies. The opposition Paul faced is typical in churches everywhere.

Christians will face opposition on occasions, but they must minister according to the ministry God gives them. Paul explained in his letter to the Church at Rome. Paul said:

> Let us use it in our ministering; he who teaches, in teaching; he who exhorts, in exhortation; he who gives, with liberality; he who leads, with diligence; he who shows mercy, with cheerfulness. (Romans 12:7-8)

Christians minister with their financial resources and according to the Bible it ought to be liberal giving.

God is the source of all financial wealth or lack thereof. "The LORD makes poor and makes rich; He brings low and lifts up" (1 Samuel 2:7). "The rich and the poor have this in common, the LORD is the maker of them all" (Proverbs 22:2). Those who have financial resources are ministers of God's grace. However, financial wealth may cause unfaithfulness. "But woe to you who are rich, for you have received your consolation" (Luke 6:24). The story or parable in the gospel of Luke is an eye-opener (Luke 16:19-31).

Christians are managers of God's estate; All the material blessings, land, money, possessions belong to God. Christians simply manage them the few years they have on earth. The parable in Luke 16 explains how two very different men lived while in the earthly body and what happened when these two men left the earthly body.

In this life God granted the rich man a very wealthy estate. Wealth is not a sin. Abraham was rich and so was King David and many other godly men. Wealth may be used for God's glory or man's glory. In this life the rich man's wealth made him feel important - so important that he was in love with himself. In this life he ate the most expensive meals, dressed in the finest clothing and lived in dazzling spender day in and day out. He was satisfied with his material wealth.

The other man in this story was poor, in fact a beggar. He was homeless, afflicted with a disease and was eager to be fed with the scraps that came from the rich man's table. In this life having dogs come and lick his sores further shamed the poor beggar. In this life, one man had it made. In this life, the other man was considered an outcast. Jesus has already made a contrast with these two men in a previous sermon. "Blessed are the poor and hungry" but "woe to those rich and well fed" (Luke 6:20—26).

In the course of time the beggar died and was carried away by the angels to Abraham's bosom. While he was on earth he put his trust in God and now God had ordered the angels to take his soul to paradise. The other man died and was buried. Maybe it was a splendid burial but angels did not meet his soul.

The Lord specifically mentioned the burial. The Lord intended to show us the difference between the shadow and reality. Rituals varied in the ancient culture, but one aspect of the funeral was consistent. The length of time for which a body was displayed depended largely on his position. A poor man would usually be buried the same day he died, whereas the rich and famous were on display for up to a week. People were admiring, mourning, and honoring the dead body of the rich man who was at that time in Hell. The body of Lazarus was forgotten, but he was in the glorious presence of the Lord.

Human life and this present world are quickly passing away, but there is another place after humans leave this world. Luke's parable reveals the reversal of roles. The wealthy, self-centered, live it up rich man in this world becomes the poor, miserable, and despised beggar in the next life. The poor beggar in this world becomes rich in all things, honorable and happy in the next life.

The text in Luke's gospel should remind Christians that liberal giving is eternally important and conservative hoarding is eternally ignominious. Paul's letter to the Corinthians is an appeal for all Christians to minister with liberal giving.

Paul's challenge to the Corinthian Church is to complete the collection for the church at Jerusalem. Paul remembered the admonition of the Jerusalem council to "remember the poor" (Galatians 2:10). The opponents of Paul at Corinth had successfully distracted the Corinthian Christians away from the collection, which Paul had previously called to the attention of the Corinthian church. "Now concerning the collection for the saints, as I have given orders to the churches of Galatia, so you must do also" (1 Corinthians 16:10).

This particular portion of God's word is more concerned with the grace of giving than with the management of finances in the church.

Paul referred to the church members at Corinth in terms of "brethren." This is a term of endearment. Paul's approach to the subject of giving may be misunderstood as "intimidation." For instance, he was rather straight forward with Philemon: "Receive Onesimus like you would me. If he owes anything, I'll pay it, but remember brother "you owe me even your own self" (Philemon 19). However, Paul makes an appeal to the brothers.

Paul compared the Corinthian Christians with the Macedonian Christians. The Macedonian churches were pushed to the edge with afflictions. Christians today do not know the extent of their suffering, but what they do know and understand is that "in a great trial of affliction the abundance of their joy and their deep poverty abounded in the riches of their liberality" (2 Corinthians 8:2).

The Macedonian churches were impoverished because of wars, barbarian invasion and the empty gold mines that once flourished in that region. The Macedonians were poor in comparison to their Corinthian counterparts, but they were rich in their giving. The Bible describes them as people of great generosity.

The question is: Why was the giving so great in a city that was so impoverished and the giving so little in a city of wealth and prosperity? The Macedonian Christians had a right view of their relationship with Christ. They understood and had experienced the grace of God. The generosity of the Macedonian Christians was not self induced. God gave them grace and the Macedonians were delighted to show that grace. The Macedonians were generous beyond our understanding when we see the outward circumstances militating against their generosity.

God uses afflictions, trials, persecution and poverty to show His strength in situations that seem humanly impossible. Christians should take heart and learn from the great generosity of the Macedonians. Their generosity required a sacrifice. They gave beyond their ability (2 Corinthians 8:3).

Many Christians today are of the Corinthian variety. They give out of their wealth rather than out of their poverty. Christians ought to study the full counsel of God.

Now Jesus sat opposite the treasury and saw how the people put money into the treasury. And many who were rich put in much. Then one poor widow came and threw in two mites, which make a *quadrans* (one cent). So He called His disciples to Himself and said to them, "Assuredly, I say to you that this poor widow has put in more than all those who have given to the treasury; for they all put in out of their abundance, but she out of her poverty put in all that she had, her whole livelihood." (Mark 12:41-44)

It does not matter whether Christians are rich or poor; they should give liberally to God's work. The generosity of the Macedonians was also accompanied by a sense of privilege. The Macedonian churches urged Paul to "receive the gift and the fellowship of the ministering to the saints" (2 Corinthians 8:4). The Greek word *charis* translated "gift" in verse four could be translated "grace." Now isn't that a novel idea - the grace of ministering. The generosity of the Macedonian's was a ministry to the saints. Their affection for the saints in Jerusalem was a copy of the grace that God had shown to the Macedonians. The grace of God draws a person close to God. A theological term that describes a peculiar closeness to God is "the blessing of God."

When Christians are near the Lord in fellowship, it will be expressed in their love for each other. The sacrificial and generous giving of the Macedonians gave Paul every reason to encourage the Corinthians to fulfill their responsibility to Christ. As Christians think about their eternal estate, they should also remember their responsibilities in their secular estate. "But as you abound in everything – in faith, in speech, in knowledge, in all diligence, and in your love for us – see that you abound in this grace also" (2 Corinthians 8:7).

15 Stewardship by Comparison

2 Corinthians 8:8-15

The ministry of stewardship is a reflection of Christian love for God and for one another. Paul applies this principle in his letter to the Corinthians. The collection for the impoverished saints at Jerusalem was evidence of Christian love. Paul gave specific instructions in his first letter to the Corinthians.

> Now concerning the collection for the saints, as I have given orders to the churches of Galatia, so you must do also: On the first day of the week let each one of you lay something aside, storing up as he may prosper, that there be no collections when I come. (1 Corinthians 16:1-2)

There have been some wild expositions come from this text. Pastors and church leaders may try to use this text to prove that tithing to the church is a New Testament commandment. There is a difference between a New Testament principle and a New Testament commandment. The word tithe is only found in the New Testament as an Old Testament directive.

A brief explanation of the tithe is necessary to understand Paul's ministry to the Corinthians. The word tithe simply means a tenth. In Holy Scripture it means giving one-tenth of the increase of property.

In Leviticus 27:30-33 the Old Testament church was required to tithe the seed, corn, wine, oil, and fruit. So, whether a person made ten bushels of corn or one hundred bushels of corn ten percent belonged to the Lord. It may help to mention the radical contrast of God's law compared to man's law. Under the Old Testament theocracy (God's rule over state/church), total giving to the church/state was ten percent. There is a distinct difference between a tyranny and a tithe.

The tithe was required for religious and charitable uses in the Old Testament church. The tithe was divided three ways.

1) The Levitical Tithe was for the Levites. The Levites were the ministers set apart for the spiritual welfare of the Old Testament congregation. They were not assigned any land, they didn't have any inheritance, but they did have homes assigned to them with sufficient space for a garden. The Levites were to be properly supported by the tithes of the Old Testament congregation so they would not have to set aside their spiritual callings for secular work. The principle of the tithe was simple. Ten families should be able to support one family.

2) The Sanctuary Tithe was a tithe set aside for use when the adult males attended the religious feasts at Jerusalem. The tithe was to be used for their expenses when they attended the Passover or Pentecost or some other annual feast.

3) The Poor Tithe was used for charitable uses. We should note that the tithe for the poor was administered by the individual family and not by the church corporately.

The principle of the tithe set forth by Moses is extremely important for the New Testament church.

> You shall truly tithe all the increase of your grain that the field produces year by year. And you shall eat before the LORD your God, in the place where He chooses to make His name abide, the tithe of your grain and your new wine and your oil, of the firstborn of your herds and your flocks, that you may learn to fear the LORD your God always. But if the journey is too long for you, so that you are not able to carry the tithe, or if the place where the

LORD your God chooses to put His name is too far from you, when the LORD your God has blessed you, then you shall exchange it for money, take the money in your hand, and go to the place which the LORD your God chooses. And you shall spend that money for whatever your heart desires: for oxen or sheep, for wine or similar drink, for whatever your heart desires; you shall eat there before the LORD your God, and you shall rejoice, you and your household. You shall not forsake the Levite who is within your gates, for he has no part nor inheritance with you. At the end of every third year you shall bring out the tithe of your produce of that year and store it up within your gates. And the Levite, because he has no portion nor inheritance with you, and the stranger and the fatherless and the widow who are within your gates, may come and eat and be satisfied, that the LORD your God may bless you in all the work of your hand which you do. (Deuteronomy 14:22-29)

The question may immediately arise, "what about the maintenance of the building, commonly called the Temple at Jerusalem?" There was no portion of the tithe especially set aside for building maintenance. (That may come as a shock to some Christians, especially those who love the building). The tithes were not used to maintain the church building. The Temple was to be maintained by free will offerings. For instance, late in the history of the Old Testament, Ezra makes reference to the "freewill offerings for the house of God which is in Jerusalem" (Ezra 1:4). The Old Testament tithe is a principle that New Testament Christians must not ignore, but the tithe is a principle not a mandate.

When Paul told the Corinthian Christians to set aside whatever they had prospered, there was no limit set. So how should Christians be good stewards of the things God has entrusted to them? The concept involved in biblical stewardship is best understood when Christians make comparisons, and that is what I mean when I titled this chapter "Stewardship by Comparison."

First and most important we have to compare the grace of God in the Old Testament to the grace of God in the New Testament. God's grace in the Old Testament was seen through the eyes of the Old Testament saint by means of types, figures and copies. For instance, the ceremonial laws all pointed to the grace of God's forgiveness in Jesus Christ.

God's grace to the Old Testament saint was sufficient for salvation because of the mere promise. However, the New Testament saint could not deny that God has shown more grace to the New Testament saint through the humiliation and exaltation of Jesus Christ. Who understands the grace of God clearer, the Old Testament saint who only saw the sacrifice of a mediator through the blood of bulls and goats or the New Testament saint who sees the sacrifice through the blood of Jesus Christ, the God-man? God's people in the Old Testament looked forward to the Messiah. The grace necessary for forgiveness of sins was sufficient in the Old Testament just as it is today, but New Testament saints are graced with a fresher and clearer understanding of God's saving grace.

The reader may be asking, "what does God's saving grace have to do with the grace of giving?" The grace of giving under the Old Testament law was ten percent, but now the grace of giving, like the grace of salvation, should be seen as a ministry rather than a duty. That is the reason that Paul said by inspiration "see that you abound in this grace" [the grace of giving] (2 Corinthians 8:7).

Christians show the evidence of God's grace through their giving. A minister serves and that applies to giving. If giving is a measure of grace, who denies himself or herself one luxury or refuses one indulgence that he or she may have the means of contributing more to the cause of the Redeemer? How many give only what they think they will not miss? Are such gifts sacrifices, and is it any wonder the alleged gift should stink in the nostrils of the Lord of hosts.

Christians must prove the reality of their love (2 Corinthians 8:8). Paul told the Corinthian Church that the Macedonian Christians gave beyond their ability in the face of trials and afflictions (2 Corinthians 8:1-4). Then Paul compares the Macedonian Christians to the church at Corinth. The apostle does not intend to encourage competition or contention, but the apostle reminds the Corinthians to compare the grace that God had shown them to the grace that God had shown the Macedonians. Apparently the grace of giving abounded among the Macedonians. Should the grace of giving abound with the Corinthian Christians? They had more financial resources than the Macedonians. Should the grace of giving abound from New Testament Christians?

The apostle made comparisons throughout his exposition for the purpose of instruction and worship. As God teaches us how to be good stewards of the things he has loaned us in this life, we should respond with worship to the giver of all gifts.

Stewardship by comparison is evident throughout Paul's letter to the Corinthians. "For you know the grace of our Lord Jesus Christ, that though He was rich, yet for your sakes He became poor, that you through His poverty might become rich" (2 Corinthians 8:9). Paul compares the beginning of the Corinthian ministry with the end of the ministry (2 Corinthians 8:10 -11). Paul compares one's ability to give (2 Corinthians 8:12). Interestingly enough, Paul's comparisons end in equality (2 Corinthians 8:14).

The notion of equality has nothing to do with communism. Jerusalem was the mother church of all the mission churches at that time. For various reasons and some of those reasons may have been ambitious misgivings, the church at Jerusalem was in need. The saints of God should supply her needs, not with a tithe, but with a heart filled with Jesus Christ who gave everything for God's children.

The worldly possessions of the Corinthians should have been viewed as the Macedonian Christians viewed them. In the end, there will be no comparisons of who has what and who does what. In the end, Christians are all equal before God. He will judge them, not on the merits of their worldly possessions, but they will be judged on the merits of Jesus Christ applied to their souls.

16 Stewardship is Honorable

2 Corinthians 8:16-24

The apostle Paul is the sterling example of a man who understood the Christian religion from its essential foundation to every aspect of Christianity's noble fulfillment in the lives of men and women. The apostle was a man of distinction and conviction with the capacity for understanding the great or the small. He loved those of the faith and was fearless of those who despised the faith.

Paul's concern for the saints at Corinth is a remarkable example of his ministry. There were a few troublemakers at Corinth (and every church has its share of troublemakers). The troublemakers tried to influence the Corinthians to believe a false gospel. The gospel is *Theocentric* (God-centered), *bibliocentric* (Bible-centered), and *Christocentric* (Christ-Centered). The gospel is not unrelated to Christian character in the wide sense of the word. Jesus said if you love me keep my commandments (John 14:15). The gospel encompasses much more than a brief explanation of God's saving grace.

Paul wrote the Philippian Church and said, "Only let your conduct be worthy of the gospel of Christ" (Philippians 1:27). The great apostle realized that the gospel was more than a profession of faith. Paul took his ministry very seriously and was not afraid to stand against those who might disgrace or degrade the gospel. He was not afraid of his enemies at Corinth, but his primary interest was the souls of the saints at Corinth and by extension the pastoral ministry of every church. The faithful ministry of a minister ought to be fearless of the enemy, but faithful to the elect of God so they will reflect the integrity towards the gospel. The integrity of the gospel should be the primary focus of any minister. The ministers I have in mind are those who serve Jesus Christ through the ministry of the church.

To put it another way, every member of the church should focus their attention on the integrity of the gospel. Sometimes church members are called hypocrites. When that happens, whether it is true or not, the integrity of the gospel has come into question. The integrity of the gospel is relative to the full counsel of God. Therefore, financial stewardship is related to the gospel and becomes an important doctrine in Paul's letter to the Corinthians.

Titus was an important minister to Paul's gospel ministry. Paul sent Titus to Corinth to collect the gift for the saints in Jerusalem. Titus was a man that could be trusted or otherwise Paul would not have entrusted Titus with a financial gift. There are two unnamed companions with Titus.

For some reason Paul makes much to do over the credentials of these three men. Paul wanted to stress the integrity of the men, thus the integrity of the gospel. Integrity is very important when money is involved. Unfortunately, many who profess the name of Christ cannot be trusted with church finances.

Sometimes one or more individuals in the church want to control the finances of the church. Sometimes that zeal for control calls the integrity of the gospel in question. Paul commended the integrity of Titus and his companions so, "that anyone should blame us in this lavish gift which is administered by us"(2 Corinthians 8:20). Paul did not want anyone to have a reason to question his integrity, since he was probably handling large sums of money. It would be nice if all Christians took that attitude, rather than take the attitude that they are in control of God's money.

Christians should understand the temporary ministry of financial stewardship, because in the end God will dispose of all earthly wealth, even every atomic particle. Christian ministers ought to search the Scriptures to determine God's gift and what God expects of them. Jesus said, "For everyone to whom much is given, from him much will be required" (Luke 12:48). What you possess is irrelevant in the eyes of God, except that you have enough to meet your needs. What you do with what you possess is to the point of Paul's letter to the Corinthians.

Stewardship is honorable. Stewardship is related to management. In the context of Paul's letter to the Corinthians, stewardship has to do with the management of financial resources. The management of money that God provides for the advancement of His kingdom is an honorable ministry. Paul said, "providing honorable things, not only in the sight of the Lord, but also in the sight of men" (2 Corinthians 8:21).

The Greek word *kalos* is translated "honorable" in the *New King James* text. "It means good, not so much in the sense of an ethical evaluation as in that of pleasant, enjoyable beneficial, what is pleasing to Yahweh, what he likes or what gives him joy" (*Dictionary of New Testament Theology*, vol. 2, p. 103). The *New International Version* gives the word "honorable" a little different twist to make it a bit more readable. It reads, "For we are taking pains to do what is right, not only in the eyes of the Lord but also in the eyes of men." To put that in perspective, the honorable thing was/is the right thing in the presence of God and men.

Honesty is always honorable. A crucial and absolutely essential mark of a Christian is honesty. Contrary to honesty is dishonesty. Paul's opponents at Corinth were dishonest, because they had a false gospel. An honest person always stands out. A dishonest person will soon be known by his or her doctrine and life. Dishonesty is an infectious condition that plagues the church and casts a dark shadow on the truth of the gospel. Unbelievers are quick to point out how dishonest a Christian may have conducted himself or herself.

Christian ministers would be wise to learn and understand the biblical teaching on dishonesty and actually it is quite simple. Inclination to dishonesty begins at an early age, because it is merely the actualization of original sin. After Adam and Eve sinned against God and broke covenant with God, there was an immediate dishonest response.

God asked Adam, "have you eaten from the tree of which I commanded you that you should not eat?"

Then the man said, "The woman whom you gave to be with me she gave me of the tree and I ate." (Genesis 3:11-12)

Adam was dishonest by trying to blame his sin on everybody else. Dishonesty is not just an American tradition, although there is plenty of it around. Dishonesty prevails because it has been accepted as a cultural world and life view. Many people think dishonesty is natural and therefore it must be acceptable.

There are many reasons that dishonesty is widely accepted among Christians. It may be the result of dishonest parents or dishonest employers. Shrewd dealings are learned at a very early age. Excessive debt is encouraged from the earliest age. The desire for things of the world is a major source of dishonesty.

Dishonesty is not just learned behavior, it is a condition of the heart that appears on two fronts. Honesty or dishonesty will find an audience in the sight of man. The Word of God calls for honesty in the sight of men. The way Christians act and speak relative to truth is important to the integrity of the gospel. They will do well to remember Paul's admonition to the church: "abstain from the form of evil" (1 Thessalonians 5:22). The word "form" in that text is derived from the Greek word *eiddos* which literally referred to "that which is seen" thus the appearance of evil. Paul knew that his opponents at Corinth would be ready to condemn him by spreading the rumor that Paul used the funds for himself. For that reason Paul had to be extra careful before men.

The Word of God also calls for honesty before God. It is possible for a man to get away with some dishonest measure, but ultimately God sees it and God will judge the sinner. It will be a horrible judgment for those without Christ. There is grace and forgiveness with Christ.

God will approve or disapprove of all ministries, including stewardship. There are those in the church who do not fear God. They act as if this life will terminate all senses and essences of existence. Paul's letter to the Corinthians disproves any such idea. When Christians speak of being in the sight of the Lord, they speak in terms of God's eternal existence. To put it another way, there is no way of escaping the eyes of God, now or ever.

Maybe that is the reason Paul chooses his words carefully. Paul's emphasis is on the administration of the gift. The word administration comes from a Greek word, which means "to manage." God gives managerial responsibility over a certain domain. Christians are merely managers and in the end will have to give an account to God as to how they have managed His resources.

Christians will do well to read Jesus' parable of the talents (Matthew 25:14-30). That parable ends with these awful words: "cast the unprofitable servant into the outer darkness. There will be weeping and gnashing of teeth" (Matthew 25:30). However, poor stewardship and bad management is not the unforgivable sin. God's grace is abundant. If Christians are uncertain about their stewardship, that is whether or not it is honorable stewardship, they should cast themselves upon the grace and mercy of God.

If God is pleased to pour out his grace and mercy, then remember the words of the Apostle Paul. "Therefore show to them, and before the churches, the proof of your love and of our boasting on your behalf" (2 Corinthians 8:24). It will show that stewardship is honorable.

17 How Much is Enough?

2 Corinthians 9:1-15

Martin Luther once said the Bible could be divided into two parts: the law and the gospel. Luther is right in principle, but in practice Christians often divide the Bible into two parts: morality and immorality. It is easy to be distracted from the law and gospel. Likewise, it is so easy to turn stewardship, especially financial giving, into a moral lesson.

A careful study of the Word of God requires a careful study of the words in the Word of God. For instance, Paul said, "Thanks be to God for His indescribable gift!" (2 Corinthians 9:15). Indescribable fails the test of common language at this point. Something that is indescribable cannot be described. The translators refer to God's indescribable gift. How do we know it is a gift if the gift is indescribable? As always, translating from one language to another with such a vast time spread is a challenge. The New Testament was originally written in Greek nearly 2000 years ago and there are times when it is difficult to translate the words so that they make sense in modern English.

Some people could care less about the Word of God, so it doesn't matter if a word makes sense or not. Too often the only desire is a moral lesson and a moral lesson can be extracted from a corrupt translation of the Bible. The word indescribable in this context essentially means that the object cannot be fully explained or explained in detail. Luke referred to the word in Acts: "they were passing through both Phoenicia and Samaria, describing in detail the conversion of the Gentiles" (Acts 15:3). "Describing in detail" is the same word used in Paul's letter to the Corinthians, except Paul has a negation prefixed to the word, so it would say "not describing in detail."

What is the gift that cannot be described in detail? It is the forgiveness of sin by grace through faith in Christ alone. In one word the gift that cannot be fully described is the gospel. It is so wondrous and above human explanation, it is accepted by faith.

My purpose for considering the last verse first is to point out that financial stewardship is absolutely worthless without the gospel. If you are not in a right relationship with Jesus Christ, you could give your entire estate that might consist of millions of dollars. However, your money without Christ will merely soothe your conscience and divert your attention away from the coming judgment. Having said that I want to say that with Christ your giving will reflect the grace of God in you.

Our fellowship with Jesus Christ should be like the Macedonians. It must not be silent, blind or ignorant. The generous giving of the Macedonians and the expected generosity of the Corinthians said something about their fellowship with Christ or as Paul said, "the exceeding grace of God" in them.

Christians ought to think through the doctrine of stewardship and its relation to the gospel with great care. Self examination is necessary to see how much grace abounds because of the gospel. The measure of God's grace in your life may help you answer the question: How much is enough? The Word of God says, "God is able to make all grace abound toward you, that you, always having all sufficiency in all things, may have an abundance for every good work."

When you ask the question "how much should I give" you must ask, how much grace has God given me. It is possible to have the gospel and not have an understanding of what God requires of His people. Christians must understand that financial stewardship is directly related to the gospel. However, the New Testament does not use the word tithe in the sense of establishing the amount Christians give toward church related ministry.

The prosperity gospel is popular among many celebrity preachers and teachers. Their fundamental doctrine is the more you give the more you get in return. They believe Paul taught the prosperity gospel in his letter to the Corinthians. "But this I say:

He who sows sparingly will also reap sparingly, and he who sows bountifully will also reap bountifully" (2 Corinthians 9:6). The Word of God is true and the principle found in vs. 6 is true. The laws of harvest are natural as well as spiritual, but there is a distinction. Let's say I sow 10 seeds and you sow 100 seeds. Who will have the bigger crop? You don't have to be a genius to figure out that the more seed you plant the more plants you will have to harvest from if there are no intervening historical contingencies such as a natural catastrophe. However, what if you get a hailstorm on your 100 plants and 90% of them are killed? If my 10 seeds are fruitful to harvest, who has the bigger harvest?

The mechanics of the law of sowing and reaping is simple enough. Paul told the Galatian church that whatever a man sows, that he will also reap (Galatians 6:7-8). Jesus said, "Give, and it will be given to you; good measure, pressed down, shaken together, and running over" (Luke 6:38). However, the principle of sowing and reaping does not set a specific amount.

The 10% principle does not fit into Paul's teaching on the subject of financial stewardship. If Christians meticulously tithe, where is grace and what is the internal state of the giver's heart?

The sowing and harvesting principle in verse six may be misunderstood without bringing verse seven into the immediate context. "So let each one give as he purposes in his heart, not grudgingly or of necessity; for God loves a cheerful giver" (2 Corinthians 9:7).

Generous giving is closely associated with cheerful giving. Again the amount is not the issue. In his first letter to the Corinthian church Paul said, "let each one of you, lay something aside, storing up as he may prosper" (1 Corinthians 16:2). You can almost hear the joy of giving according to the Lord's grace. This reminds me of the building of the temple. "Then the leaders of the fathers' houses, leaders of the tribes of Israel, the captains of thousands and of hundreds, with the officers over the king's work, offered willingly" (1 Chronicles 29:6). They were not giving to the Lord's work by compulsion. They found joy in giving as we note from the words of King David.

> O Lord our God, all this abundance that we have prepared to build You a house for Your holy name is from Your hand, and is all Your own. I know also, my God, that You test the heart and have pleasure in uprightness. As for me, in the uprightness of my heart I have willingly offered all these things. (1 Chronicles 29:16)

The offerings were given freely and joyously. The Old Covenant believers were "heart givers" so Paul told the Corinthians, "give as he purposes in his heart" (2 Corinthians 9:7). Paul used the word "purposes" to explain "what one decides." It is a heart decision. Some heart decisions are good and some are bad. Ananias and Sapphira made a heart decision, but it was a bad decision (See Acts 5:1-11). Selfishness took control even though they had decided in their heart to give. The spirit of covetousness is a heart problem.

How much is enough?

1. There is no quota system in the New Testament doctrine of giving, because it is by God's grace that all your needs are supplied.

2. Giving financially according to biblical doctrine is a ministry of stewardship.

3. The church gives according to God's grace, not according to God's law. The Lord Jesus Christ became poor so that we might be rich in His grace.

4. The church gives, not under compulsion, or by necessity, but freely and generously according to the grace of God in the gospel of Jesus Christ.

18 Christian Worldview Ministry

2 Corinthians 10:1-6

Paul had a passion for the souls of those professing Christians at Corinth. Paul reveals his personal interest in the Corinthian Christians even sacrificing good grammar to get his point across. "I, Paul, myself" was an expression of emphasis on his relationship with the Corinthian church. His speech is that of a humble servant of Christ. Paul encouraged the Corinthians with meekness and gentleness, even the meekness and gentleness of Christ.

However, in the same breath he appears to speak irony or what some people might call sarcasm. Paul describes himself as being timid in person, but bold at a safe distance away. I say it is sarcasm, because Paul does not exhibit a countenance of timidity in the New Testament. In fact, when he entered into a new city, his gospel boldness lands him some jail time or either a beating. Paul does not sound like a timid man. So, it appears that Paul has someone specific in mind when he referred to being "lowly among you, but bold in his absence."

Paul refers to a select group of people when he said, "I intend to be bold against some" (2 Corinthians 10:2). He probably has his opponents in mind or perhaps some unrepentant church members who were followers of Paul's opposition party. In any case, Paul repeats what he had heard and the opponents had said, "some, who think of us as if we walked according to the flesh" (2 Corinthians 10:2). The effort by Paul's opponents was to make Paul appear like a worldly minded man, a man acting according to the standards of this world.

Some people have a unique, but devilish ability to make something appear to be contrary to its true nature. Con artists employ that tactic all the time to manipulate people. Christians should be able to think above those who try to manipulate with fideism and sophism.

Paul went to the Corinthians with meekness and gentleness because he was a product of the gospel of Jesus Christ. Our appearance and our actions are a result of what we are. I am a Christian therefore I will act, in some sense and to some degree, like Jesus Christ.

To put it another way the gospel has changed my soul, my soul has changed my thinking, and my thinking has changed my choices. It is called a world and life view. Our nation and many churches are engaged in a labyrinth of culture wars. These wars are being fought in the public arena over politics, law, education, and various other important issues. These cultural wars began over opposing views of a philosophy of life.

The apostle Paul warns Christians not to be taken captive through philosophy and empty deception (Colossians 2:8). The word "philosophy" refers to one who is a friend of wisdom. Paul also says, "walk not as fools but as wise" (Ephesians 5:15). Christians must not be taken captive to vain philosophy and Christians should not be silent. However, John Calvin warned, "Silence in the church is the banishment and crushing of the truth." Yet the Christians who are the most vocal seem to be right at home using language like "I feel" or "I believe" without any reference to truth. Better to be a student of godly philosophy pursuing the truth, than a student of the Bible and teach false doctrine (Ezekiel 33:1-11). There have been numerous polls asking if Christians believe in absolute truth. Many of the polls reveal that the majority of Christians do not believe there is absolute truth. If there is no absolute truth, there are no moral absolutes.

The New age philosophy that denies absolute truth is a popular trend in many churches in North America. It appears many people are losing control of their lives, by their expressions and actions. When things seem to be out of control it is time for Christians to stop and take a look at themselves. They need to look at the world around them. They need to minister with a world and life view based on the Word of God.

Paul explains the place of ministry in his letter to the Corinthians. "For though we walk in the flesh, we do not war according to the flesh" (2 Corinthians 10:3). The phrase "in flesh" is used over fifty times in the New Testament. The phrase "according to flesh" is used over twenty times in the New Testament. This is the only place in the Bible both are used in same verse. To sort this out refer to the Greek words *en sarki* (in flesh) and in this context refers to a locative of sphere, thus it shows location. The Greek words *kata sarka* (according to flesh) refers to a relationship. These two phrases "in flesh" and "according to flesh" show the antithesis of living in this world, but not living according to the patterns of this world. "In the flesh" often refers to the physical presence, therefore "in the flesh" is temporary. The place you live and minister is a temporary arrangement, because you are "in the flesh." Being "in the flesh" should cause you to take a good look at yourself. While you are in the flesh consider your present limitations in the present world. While you are in the flesh you must consider the weakness in your Christian walk (See Romans 7:14-25). While you are in the flesh you must consider your liability to error. Do not despair when you examine yourself, just be aware of your short-comings in the flesh - in the world where you live and minister.

The Christian world and life view is not a utopian perfection. Your world and life view is directly related to the fact that you are in the flesh. Even though you live in this world (in the flesh) you must not formulate a world and life view from this world's perspective (according to flesh). God has not made a mistake. Christians understand who they are before God, because the law condemns them, but the gospel of Christ by the power of the Holy Spirit saves them. Why? So they will love God and desire to keep the law of God. Therefore, in the flesh, they will formulate a world and life view based on the Word of God.

Since all Christians have a ministry in the gospel, they all have the powers available to formulate a Christian world and life view. "For the weapons of our warfare are not carnal but mighty in God for pulling down strongholds" (2 Corinthians 10:4). There are many obstacles that prevent Christians from formulating a Christian world and life view so they need power to perform ministry.

The obstacles express themselves when Satan's warriors attack the unsuspecting pilgrim. It is natural for Satan to attack the weakest point. Since human beings are rational creatures, Satan will often attack the intellect. We know that "the god of this world has blinded the minds of the unbelieving" (2 Corinthians 4:4) but he will also try to mislead the elect (Matthew 24:24). God's truth gets to the heart through the head and that is why Satan will try to blind the understanding so that one cannot judge rightly throwing him or her into confusion. Satan will also use moral depravity to cripple Christian ministers.

There is only one power that will overcome these obstacles and that power must come from the Lord God omnipotent. The power described in our text is, "mighty in God" or "divinely powerful" according to the *New American Standard Bible*. Power and strength comes from the hand of God and that is directly opposite of the weakness of the hand of Satan.

The Spirit of God works in the whole being (mind, will and emotions) as the source of power to overcome human cleverness. The Spirit of God works in us as the source of our power to overcome the things that the enemy uses against us like:

    Eloquent speech
    Powerful propaganda
    Charismatic personalities
    Managerial madness in the church
    Therapeutic thrust in the church

Satan's strongholds can be defeated when ministers of the gospel use the weapons available to them. Christians who are empowered by the Holy Spirit and equipped with the Word of God will demolish the false arguments that presume to rise up against the gospel of God. Christians are responsible for using the equipment God has given them. It will take serious inquiry into the Word of God to fight the war that is being waged by evil workers against the church of Jesus Christ.

God will protect His Christian ministers from such evil workers and empower them to clearly and cogently cast down arguments and bring every thought captive to the Word of God. They are commanded to bring every thought captive to the obedience of Christ. Therefore, they are commanded to have a Christian world and life view.

> 1. Standards to worship and serve God are established by the Word of God.
>
> 2. Destroy the false arguments raised up by the enemy of the gospel.
>
> 3. Take every thought captive to the obedience of Christ. Paul used a military metaphor that literally means to "imprison your thoughts according to the Word of God."

A Christian world and life view is necessary to minister in this world. God will not leave His children ill-equipped for their ministry. He has given them His Word. They are commanded to use it for the glory of God.

19 Ministry by Comparison

2 Corinthians 10:7-18

Paul wrote the Corinthian Church because it was a troubled church. After nearly 2000 years the church is still troubled.

There are many suggestions, either in the form of innuendo or irony, to believe Paul had opponents at Corinth. His opponents intended to deceive the people at Corinth. For instance Paul wrote, "For we are not, as so many, peddling the Word of God" (2 Corinthians 2:17). The word "peddling" refers to something fake. Paul did not think that those who opposed him were preaching the true gospel. The apostle preached, "the fragrance of Christ among those who are being saved and among those who are perishing" (2 Corinthians 2:15). Paul defended his ministry against his opponents. Paul's opponents peddled the Word of God, but Paul preached the Word of God.

The apostle approached a troubled church with care and with a pastoral heart. The apostle said, "Not that we have dominion over your faith, but are fellow workers for your joy…" (2 Corinthians 1:24). Sometimes joy only comes when one realizes the reality of life. Joy comes from confidence, confidence comes from that which is real, and reality comes from one source and that one source is God. Christians cannot understand joy unless they have a source of ultimate authority. The apostle was a good pastor. He knew that the believers at Corinth were subject to lose sight of their ultimate authority. If they lost sight of their ultimate authority, they would have no joy in their ministry to the Lord.

Every Christian has a purpose and a ministry. Sometimes they want to minister in ways that do not fit their gifts. Sometimes they want to minister without preparation or support from the collective church. Sometimes they want to minister without any authority over them. The Word of God is clear enough on the matter and manner in which the church is prepared for ministry.

> And He Himself gave some to be apostles, some prophets, some evangelists, and some pastors and teachers, for the equipping of the saints for the work of ministry, for the edifying of the body of Christ, till we all come to the unity of the faith and of the knowledge of the Son of God, to a perfect man, to the measure of the stature of the fullness of Christ; that we should no longer be children, tossed to and fro and carried about with every wind of doctrine, by the trickery of men, in the cunning craftiness of deceitful plotting, but, speaking the truth in love, may grow up in all things into Him who is the head – Christ – from whom the whole body, joined and knit together by what every joint supplies, according to the effective working by which every part does its share, causes growth of the body for the edifying of itself in love. (Ephesians 4:11-16)

The saints (every Christian) must be prepared for "the work of ministry." The Ephesian Church was not a troubled church in the same sense that Corinth was a troubled church. The Ephesians understood the authority structure for preparing the saints for ministry. The Corinthian Church needed to hear something more authoritative. To the Corinthian Church Paul said, "The Lord gave us our authority for edification and not for your destruction." Paul was forced to exert his authority because he was attacked by worldly-minded men. When our biblical ministry is attacked by worldly unbiblical thinking, we must ask ourselves, by whose standard do we minister and serve the Lord? The answer is Jesus Christ (2 Corinthians 10:7).

Christians tend to measure their moral code according to their own inclinations. For instance, if a person thinks it is proper to murder other people for self-gain, then that person may very well join the mafia. Your own preferences will find approval with those of like mind. So the standard by which you measure your actions depends on those with whom you associate if you are inclined like they are inclined. To put it another way, it is ministry by comparison. Paul puts ministry by comparison into godly perspective. "For we dare not class ourselves or compare ourselves with those who commend themselves. But they, measuring themselves by themselves, and comparing themselves among themselves, are not wise" (2 Corinthians 10:12). Paul did not compare himself to the standards of his opponents. Paul knew very well that they were proud men tooting their own horn, bringing letters of commendation, and craftily persuading the people with their deceit. Self-praise was their standard because they did not understand a fundamental principle of the Christian religion, which is the authority of Scripture.

If a person falsely claims to be something that he or she is not, trying to measure up to their false claim is futile. Christian men and women should not try to measure up to frivolous ungodly world views. The same principle applies to Christians who say that they have done as much as the next person. Paul said "we boast not in other men's labors" (2 Corinthians 10:15). The only objective standard for all Christians is the Word of God.

The ancient Greek philosopher Protagoras said, "man is the measure of all things." God is sovereign and God has given His people His Word, so there is a sense in which the Bible is the measure of all things. The Bible does not take into account every field of science and philosophy, but the Bible does take into account the nature and character of God and what God expects from all people.

Christians must keep a right perspective. The concept of authority must not be ignored. We live in a culture that teaches neutrality, not sovereignty. It is so easy to get on the wrong road because the standard by which we measure ourselves is neither objective nor sovereign.

19 Ministry by Comparison

Those who oppose the gospel of Jesus Christ commend themselves and offend the Lord. They should listen to the wisdom of Solomon. "Let another praise you, and not your own mouth; someone else, and not your own lips" (Proverbs 27:2). Self-commendation is intolerable before the Lord. Jesus told the parable of the Pharisee and Tax Collector which demonstrates ministry by comparison.

> Two men went up to the temple to pray, one a Pharisee and the other a tax collector. The Pharisee stood and prayed thus with himself, God I thank You that I am not like other men - extortioners, unjust, adulterers, or even as this tax collector. I fast twice a week; I give tithes of all that I possess. And the tax collector standing afar off, would not so much as raise his eyes to heaven, but beat his breast, saying God be merciful to me a sinner. I tell you this man went down to his house justified rather than the other for everyone who exalts himself will be humbled, and he who humbles himself will be exalted. (Luke 18:10-14)

Ministry by comparison is useful and valid if the servant of God compares his or her words and action to the Word of God.

20 Image is not Everything

2 Corinthians 11:1-15

The prominent theologian, Dr. R. C. Sproul, produced a video series for teaching young people entitled "Image is Everything." It was an interesting title because it was a title of irony. His theme was, "what you see is not necessarily what you get." Every Christian should plant that thought deep in to the crevices of the mind, because it is so true.

The context of Paul's letter to the Corinthian Church reveals his deep concern for the spiritual welfare of the Christians at Corinth. Paul said, "I am jealous for you with godly jealousy" (2 Corinthians 11:2). Jealousy is a sin and there is no reason to believe that Paul intended to sin. Paul merely expressed God's attitude for His people. Paul was the spiritual father of the Corinthians in one sense, but the Lord God is the true Father of all Christians. Therefore, the apostle wants to treat the people at Corinth, just as God the Father would treat them.

Paul spoke about the most intimate of all human relationships, which is the relationship of the husband and wife (2 Corinthians 11:2). Adam and Eve had a unique relationship with God and with each other before the fall. After the fall everything changed. Eve was deceived by the craftiness of Satan. Paul was fearful that just as Satan deceived Eve by his craftiness, that the Corinthians might be deceived. The imagery associated with Satan's deceit shows that image is not everything.

God created a perfect environment for Adam and Eve. Everything was real. The imagery Satan portrayed was his charm; it persuaded Eve that image was everything. Satan, the craftiest con-artist in the world, used a serpent to deceive Eve. Satan promoted a pro-self, anti-God agenda. Satan communicated an image of human ability and casted doubt that God's Word was true. After the deception, the eyes of Adam and Eve were opened and they knew that they were naked. The reality that once existed now looked different to Adam and Eve. The way they perceived themselves changed. Before they sinned, they saw everything the way God saw it, and that was good. After the fall, the image replaced reality.

What did Adam and Eve do to overcome this image problem? "They sewed fig leaves together and made themselves loin coverings." This is an image of two people trying to hide from God and from each other. People have been trying to do that ever since Adam and Eve. People want to hide from one another. They want to wear a mask. It seems as if it is natural for human beings to cast an image and try to cover up reality. Why do you think that people say, "Leave me alone." What they most often mean is, "do not try to step inside and see my life for what it is really like."

Sinful creatures without the renewing of the mind tend to believe, "image is everything." The truth is that since sin entered into the world, people tend to hide behind an image. To put it another way, image replaced reality. However, image is not everything. Only to the extent that the image corresponds to reality is there any substance to the image.

Paul's concern was that the Corinthians should not be deceived by his opponents, just as Eve was deceived by the serpent. He loved the Christians at Corinth too much to let that happen. Paul's opponents accused him of lacking the skills of rhetoric. Paul's response was, "Even though I am untrained in speech, yet I am not untrained in knowledge." For many public speakers, image is everything and content is nothing. To put it another way truth has been replaced by rhetoric. Christians must not be afraid to say that image is not everything.

Paul's opponents continued to put him down by creating a false image of Paul. Apparently, Paul's opponents told the Corinthian Christians that Paul should not be trusted because his preaching was free. Similar to modern times, Paul lived when certain people made their money by making speeches. The

Greeks considered skilled rhetoricians (public speakers) and philosophers like professional men. They sold their thoughts and speech for money. A philosopher who did not charge was considered a worthless philosopher and not worthy of attention. Paul's response was to bring the attention of the Corinthians to the ethics of the matter. So Paul says, "is it a sin to preach the gospel free of charge?" Paul's opponents tried to paint an image of the apostle that did not fit reality. However, the apostle charged the Corinthians to remember that image is not everything (2 Corinthians 11:7-9).

Paul's ministry was under attack by "false apostles, deceitful workers, transforming themselves into apostles of Christ" (2 Corinthians 11:13). They were in the church to disturb the peace. Jesus said, "false prophets will rise and show great signs and wonders to deceive, if possible, even the elect" (Matthew 24:24). False teachers in the church will be with us to the end. The last book of the Bible reveals the false apostles that set themselves up at Ephesus (Revelation 2:2).

False teachers change their appearance, because their father Satan changes his appearance into an angel of light.

> For Satan himself transforms himself into an angel of light. Therefore it is no great thing if his ministers also transform themselves into ministers of righteousness, whose end will be according to their works. (2 Corinthians 11:14-15)

If Satan can deceive Christians with his image and his angels can deceive Christians with their image then, the servants of Satan can surely put on the appearance of righteous men. Therefore, a bad man can put on the semblance of a godly man.

The church will be a mixture of wheat and tares according the words of the Lord Jesus Christ (Matthew 13:24-30). Yes, Satan, his angels, and his servants may have the outward appearance of good, but in the end they will get what they deserve.

> Question:
> Is Image Everything?
>
> The Answer:
> From Satan's perspective image is everything.
> From God's perspective image is NOT everything.

The world is filled with imagery of questionable reality. God's people must be discerning and cautious. Christians must be especially discerning when the gospel is the object of attention.

21 Earthly Man with a Heavenly Purpose

2 Corinthians 11:16-33

It may appear Paul temporarily ignored his own doctrine of humility. The Bible teaches that humility is a mark of the Christian. Of course the opposite of humility is pride and pride is one of the root sins. It would be obnoxious and downright sinful to believe that Paul's boasting is related to the root sin known as pride. If that was so, and it was not, the Bible would be an advocate of sinful behavior for God's people.

Paul used a form of irony in his letter to the Corinthians. For instance, if someone makes a statement which is exactly opposite of the intended meaning, it may be a statement of irony. Sometimes irony takes the form of an understatement.

Paul would never outright or by suggestion leave a Christian with the idea that boasting according to the flesh is the biblical norm. Paul wrote the Corinthian church for the purpose of defining and calling the ministers in the church to service. A minister of Christ (a servant of Christ) would never have any reason to say that Christ expects his servants to disobey. A servant of Christ is expected to obey Christ. Paul's language does not reflect disobedience, therefore he uses the language of irony to make his point.

The foolishness of self-commendation was not for the apostle Paul, because it is not according to the Lord. Self-commendation is according to the flesh. Paul used the word flesh here as he often does meaning the corrupt nature of man. The corruption is the condition inherited from Adam and is most commonly called the sin nature. The word "flesh" in Paul's vocabulary carries with it a negative connotation. To the Romans Paul said, "For I know that in me (that is, in my flesh) nothing good dwells" (Romans 7:18). To the Philippians Paul said, "to put no confidence in the flesh" (Philippians 3:3).

Paul used the words of his opponents to show the Corinthians the foolishness of listening and believing his opponents. Paul does not intend to communicate literally in this portion of his letter, because he intends to get the attention of the Corinthians for their own good. Paul was an earthly man with a heavenly purpose.

He realized that he had to live in the stench of this world and was afflicted by sinners as well as his own sin. Paul was aware of his frailty and shortcomings. He knew very well that he was a man of this earth with all the limitations of earthiness. But his purpose was heavenly. Paul had something more in mind than the foolish boasting about earthly things. His heavenly motivation was the redemption of the professing Christians in the Corinthian Church.

Paul was a minister and he expressed, "deep concern for all the churches" (2 Corinthians 11:28). The principle found throughout Scripture is that every minister has deep concern for the whole church. The principle is "serve one another." Every minister is a servant. Servants serve. Ministry takes place on earth, but if your earthly ministry does not have a heavenly purpose then your boast is according to the flesh.

If your ministry is according to the flesh, then you have been deceived by a false teacher or a deceitful worker. Those who boast according to the flesh place themselves over others as a tyrant. Such boasting is nothing but hot air. Yet, many in the church and society tolerate such tyranny. May God save you from those who boast in the flesh.

Paul has five examples of what happens when one tolerates those who boast in the flesh. "For you put up with it if one brings you into bondage, if one devours you, if one takes from you, if one exalts himself, if one strikes you on the face" (2 Corinthians 11:20).

1. The Corinthians were reduced to puppets as the boasters brought them into bondage. Paul does not

explain what brought them into bondage. The source of the power of a false teacher is by the use of words. The Corinthians were captivated by the use of words. Words may be good, but they may be very dangerous if misused. Hitler used them very effectively to control a whole nation with his deceitful tyranny.

2. The Corinthians were devoured. Paul has in mind the power deceitful workers use to get money and worldly goods. Jesus talked about the scribes as men who "devour widow's houses."

3. The Corinthians were being taken captive. They followed false teachers and deceitful workers as if though the Corinthians were slaves.

4. The Corinthians simply allowed the false teachers to exalt themselves to a position which they had no right.

5. It appears that the Corinthians even permitted physical violence. Remember the high priest commanded his men to strike Paul.

The Corinthians were no different in principle than the church today. Names, places, and circumstances change, but the same old tricks are used today. Paul admits that as God's servant he cannot justify tyranny, greed, deceit, self-exaltation and even violence. However, those false teachers and deceitful workers captivated the Corinthian Christians. Those earthly men without a heavenly purpose threatened the church.

When the church comes under attack all of God's servants should rise up to defend the church. One of the best examples in the Bible of a man who would not give in to the false teachers and deceitful workers is the apostle Paul. His defense against the wickedness of his opponents is a flagship example for all

Christians in every age (2 Corinthians 11:22-27). His defense was not boasting, but Paul declares his outward credentials. It is very likely that Paul's opponents were converted Jews since his opening statement shows his Jewish qualifications. A true minister must stand face to face with impostors in the church. Every servant of Christ will not be required to suffer the same way or even to the same degree of the apostle Paul, but I must remind you that earthly temporal suffering is part of the Christian life. The Lord Jesus said, "Remember the word that I said to you, a servant is not greater than his master. If they persecuted Me, they will also persecute you" (John 15:20).

Many of the dangers that Paul faced would come in a different way today and others will be just as the apostle faced them. There are those who claim to be among God's people, but behind your back they will cause you harm. They falsely claim to be brothers or sisters in Christ, but they want to stop the work of your ministry or in some cases it may be a vindictiveness to destroy you.

In the providence of God Christian ministers are where they are for a greater purpose than they realize. Whether you are an optimist or pessimist, if you are redeemed by the blood of Jesus Christ and adopted into the household of God, your responsibility is to be a faithful minister.

22 Work of a Minister

2 Corinthians 12:11-21

Paul's work, prayer, and passion for the saints at Corinth was the work of a minister. The most noble work of a minister is reconciliation. "Now all these things are from God, who reconciled us to Himself through Christ, and gave us the ministry of reconciliation" (2 Corinthians 5:18). The ministry of reconciliation is most often thought of as the missiological mandate. It is said from that verse that Christians must take the gospel to those without Christ on some mission field either far or near. However, that is not the context in Paul's letter to the Corinthians. Does Paul implore the Corinthians to take the gospel to Europe or England or even to Sparta just to the south of Corinth? No! Paul's interest is in the local church at Corinth.

The duties of a Christian minister are found in Scripture, but the sinful nature prefers diversions. Professing Christians often seek the place of honor rather than the humble place. They seek luxury and avoid suffering. They run from persecution and seek the praise of men.

Some professing Christians may think it sounds cozy and novel for the apostle Paul to minister to the church at the risk of humility and suffering, but then they say, "surely God would not expect me to follow in the steps of the apostle Paul." False teachers and deceitful workers would try to convince even the elect to seek honor, luxury, and praise.

Paul did not boast or brag even though he had visited paradise. Paul was bodily taken up into heaven as was Enoch and Elijah. The only difference is that Paul returned with a knowledge of heaven.

The apostle Paul had an abundance of extraordinary revelations which entitled him to a place of honor above the rest, but to protect him and literally to protect his very soul the Lord gave Paul a thorn in the flesh. Paul expressed it as a figure of speech, therefore it is difficult to determine the physical affliction. However, Paul's opponents were critical of his weaknesses, some of which may very well have been a result of the thorn in the flesh. The truth that a messenger of Satan tormented Paul is evident. The word "buffet" literally means "to beat," so that it induces pain (2 Corinthians 12:7). Satan tormented Job and perhaps it may have been a similar experience for Paul. In Paul's case he found relief by God's grace. Paul's only boast was in his weaknesses but his strength was from Christ. Paul did not boast to the Corinthians about God's grace of supernatural gifts. Neither did Paul allow his suffering to get in the way of his ministry.

Sad to say, but many ministers turn their backs on the duty of preserving integrity, maintaining biblical worship, and ministry to the church. Also, disaffected ministers in the church will begin to sow seeds of contention and discord to disturb the ministry.

Paul was the founding pastor of the church at Corinth and his love for the congregation shows as he continues to minister to their needs. Paul was about to make his third trip to Corinth. He did not want their money and he did not seek the honorable position that he was rightly due. Paul's concern was for their souls (2 Corinthians 12:15). Paul had already alluded to his relationship to the Corinthian Church being like that of a father to a son. How many fathers would seek reconciliation with their son, if the son acted like the Corinthians? These people had acted exceedingly wicked. The Corinthian Church had committed every act of vice and rebellion you could imagine. They were proud, arrogant, idolaters who committed all kinds of immoral acts. Paul explained how it was reported that a man in the church was having sex with his father's wife. In First Corinthians chapter six, Paul warned them about going to the civil court with their common disputes. Then false teachers and deceitful workers came to the church to further disturb the peace. It is in the face of such wickedness that Paul extends his love to the church, beyond what a father would extend to his own children.

Paul was willing to give of himself for the souls of those Corinthian Christians. Paul's use of the word "spend" means he is willing to spend time, money, suffer persecution, love them or whatever it takes for the church at Corinth to be restored into fellowship according to the Word of God. Further, Paul is willing to be spent which means he willing to sacrifice himself for the souls of the ministers at Corinth. Paul's interest is in bringing harmony and peace to a church that came under the influence of false teachers and deceitful workers. Such is the duty of a minister in the church.

How does a minister do his or her duty in bringing harmony and peace to the church? One way is to try to win rebellious church members back with the Word of God and biblical worship. Another way is to confront the erring sinner and urge repentance. Paul said, "I fear that when I come I shall not find you as I wish." If that sounds ambiguous Paul clears it up in vs. 21: "I am afraid that when I come, my God will again humble me before you and that I will mourn for many who have sinned earlier and not repented."

Paul thinks he may have to deal with those unrepentant and unreconciled professing church members with church discipline. The inspired apostle realized that church discipline was necessary for the spiritual good of the Corinthians. Sometimes loving someone means confronting someone with his or her sin, but always for his or her spiritual good. Paul explicitly said, "we do all things, beloved, for your edification" (2 Corinthians 12:19).

As ministers, Christians must work to strengthen each other, and therefore they will strengthen the church. Paul needed strength from the Lord to protect the gospel and preserve the integrity of the ministry of the church. Paul's language in 2 Corinthians 12:19-21 shows evidence that he fearfully expected to discipline the church when he arrived at Corinth. If the

Corinthians would not correct their own problems, the apostle would have no choice but to discipline those who were in rebellion.

The sins that Paul mentioned had created monstrous problems at Corinth. (See 2 Corinthians 12:20-21.) No doubt, Corinth was beset by sexual immorality, but the apostle has throughout his letter focused his attention on a more widespread problem and that was a divided church. Churches divide when church members allow pride to rule their lives.

Pride is a root sin that produces quarreling, jealousy, outbursts of anger, factions, slander, gossip, arrogance and finally disorder. Quarreling is nothing but contention. When the seed of contention is planted it produces jealously and then from jealousy comes anger and outrage. The party spirit clearly divides into factions. From there it is downhill until disorder consumes the church.

The only way to restore order is to obey the gospel of Jesus Christ. Jesus said, "if you love me you will keep my commandments" (John 14:15). It was Paul's desire and it should be the desire of every one of God's servants in the church to call those in sin to repentance. The apostle Paul was aware that church discipline could be avoided if those in rebellion against God's church would simply repent. The duty of every child of God (minister) is to ask forgiveness and repent.

23 Ministry of Love and Peace

2 Corinthians 13:1-14

As the apostle comes to the conclusion of his letter to the Corinthian Church, he expressed his passion for the ministry of the church. Paul ministered to the Corinthian Church because he loved to serve as a minister of Jesus Christ. "Do you not know yourselves that Jesus Christ is in you?" (2 Corinthians 13:5). Paul assumed the Corinthians had a credible profession of faith. Maybe Paul recalled the words of Jesus "I am in my Father and you are in me as I am in you" (John 14:20).

They may have been in Christ, but they apparently were not acting as if they were in Christ. There is every reason to believe that Paul had already confronted the Corinthians with their sin on a previous trip. He had certainly confronted their sins through his letters. Paul now anticipates a third trip to Corinth, but this time Paul is ready to administer discipline if necessary for the sake of those who had not repented. Paul's present warning was directed toward those who had fallen prey to the deceitful ministers. To keep this in the right perspective, the deceitful workers were a small minority, but they were deceiving the professing believers at Corinth.

Corinth is no different than many churches today. Normally one or two people will plant the seeds of contumacy. Since the sin nature is subject to deceit, contumacy rages. Contumacy is outright rebellion. It refers to people who will not listen to reason, and listens even less to the Word of God.

Christians ought to listen to this portion of Paul's letter. Paul confronted those who had sinned. If Paul had intended to speak to the whole congregation he would have said, "I write to you." This grammatical maneuver may have been on purpose. Paul may be making yet another attempt to get the congregation to discipline those in rebellion.

It is very obvious that the church did not want to discipline those rebellious people. If the Word of God is the final authority, God's people can be certain that the righteousness of Christ will be vindicated in the end. God will act decisively against those who oppose Him. There are numerous examples in Scripture that describe what happens when one acts in rebellion against God and when one rejects the authority of God. Nadab and Abihu disobeyed God in worship and the consequences were severe.

> Then Nadab and Abihu, the sons of Aaron, each took his censer and put fire in it, put incense on it, and offered profane fire before the LORD, which He had not commanded them. So fire went out from the LORD and devoured them, and they died before the LORD. (Leviticus 10:1-2)

Korah and those who followed him in rebellion were judged according to the righteousness of God (See Numbers 26:9-10).

These are merely outward examples of God's judgment against those who rebel against Him. They serve to remind us that in the end God will judge and punish all contumacy to vindicate His holiness and justice. The authority of God will not fail. It is possible that God may find more glory in the eternal damnation of an unrepentant sinner, than some outward punishment in this life. Paul's warning is for the benefit and ultimately the salvation of the souls of those rebellious professing church members at Corinth.

Paul dd not want to deal harshly with the Corinthians. He rather prefers they examine their own spiritual lives and their duty to walk with the Lord. "Examine yourselves as to whether you are in the faith. Test yourselves. Do you not know yourselves, that Jesus Christ is in you?—unless indeed you are disqualified" (2 Corinthians 13:5).

Paul encourages professing believers to examine themselves. A Christian who examines his or her own life will find plenty to work with in the way of repentance. Self-examination is nothing more or less than soul searching. To resolve sinful motives and actions privately is much preferred over a public spectacle.

However, God's people must not be distraught when the appearance of evil is present in the church. Jesus made it plain that wheat and tares would grow together. When the church began, wicked Cain was in it. When Noah's ark safely protected the visible church in the world, cursed Ham was in it. Ishmael was in the church during the life of Abraham and Esau was in the family of Issac. Even the Lord Jesus Christ permitted wicked Judas to be a part of the visible church. The visible church will never be pure in this dispensation. However, professing Christians must be faithful to examine their lives to see if Jesus Christ is present.

The Church at Corinth came face to face with division and contentions. Paul kept the right perspective by identifying those who were in Christ. Paul identifies the believing Christians at Corinth in his benediction as he did in his greeting. He called them brethren. They were also known as the saints at Corinth. The word "ministers" refers to the brethren in the church or to use Paul's term the "saints."

Every Christian has a ministry or two or three or more. As ministers in the Church of Jesus Christ, Christians serve the body of Christ so it may be made complete. Paul's prayer for the Corinthians was that the Corinthian believers would be made complete. The Greek word translated "made complete" in the *New King James Version* is translated in the *New International Version* as "perfection." Being complete or perfected refers to the reformation of those who had fallen in sin. It may be said that Paul was praying for their complete restoration so that they were no longer tossed about as children by every wind of doctrine.

Paul wanted them to repent and be restored from their state of division and contention.

The apostle Peter fell into a special and grievous sin by denying the Lord Jesus Christ three times. Peter's sin did not cause him to lose his salvation. The *Westminster Confession of Faith* explains the biblical doctrine. "The assurance true believers have of their salvation may be shaken, lessened, or interrupted for various reasons..." (*Westminster Confession of Faith*, 18.4).

Some Christians refer to this as being out of fellowship with God. Then there is the problem of broken fellowship with other Christians. The soul needs spiritual growth. Spiritual maturity is testy. Spiritual growth strains Christians, but it also tames them. The problem occurs when you stop straining, then your un-tame soul will find division and contentions as agreeable as a good steak or smoked ham. Where there is division there cannot be love and peace. As ministers in the church all of us have been called to replace division and contention with love and peace.

The inspired apostle speaks to the best interest of the believers at Corinth with the firmness that is required for sinful people. "Therefore I write these things being absent, lest being present I should use sharpness, according to the authority which the Lord has given me for edification and not for destruction" (2 Corinthians 13:10). It is very clear that Paul had the authority to discipline those who were dividing the congregation and causing all the contentions, but Paul wanted to see them grow spiritually. Paul wanted to encourage them, not destroy them. Paul's only concern was their spiritual standing before God and physical relationships in the visible church. For that reason Paul might say, "I want to build you up, not tear you down."

Paul's farewell to the ministers at Corinth ought to challenge the modern church. First, the apostle says, "become complete." This is something you must do for your self. It literally means to "reform yourself." Remember there is a prerequisite for this type of reformation. It is called justification or being in a right relationship with Jesus Christ. In the context, the Bible teaches the church at Corinth was in a state of division and contention. Those words of division and contention are translated dissension and quarreling in other translations. Paul instructed the church to be of good comfort; literally admonish yourself or persuade yourself to be of good comfort. Christians are to be of good comfort when they aim to reform themselves from the sin that causes dissension and quarreling in the body of Christ. The remedy for dissension and quarreling is to be of one mind.

> Now I exhort you brethren, by the name of our Lord Jesus Christ, that you all agree, and there be no divisions among you, but you be made complete in the same mind and in the same judgment. (1 Corinthians 1:10).

A unity of mind or a unity of opinion is absolutely necessary for the Word of God to reform the church. Christians must work through disagreements using the whole counsel of God as the standard for truth in all questions of religion.

Finally, but most important, the brethren are to live in peace. To live in peace means to have love for the brethren. Divisions and quarreling cannot and will not exist if we love each other and live in peace. The jealously and strife at Corinth caused Paul to plead with the brethren to reform themselves so they could live in peace. If Christians will do their duty, the promise is that the God of love and the God of peace will be with them.

At the time Paul wrote the Corinthians, the Jewish motif that expressed peace was that of fellowship and union based on reconciliation. The one another relationship was vitally important. Love was the foundation upon which forgiveness was built, reconciliation acknowledged and peace was the result.

Paul's benediction to the ministers at Corinth is the same benediction I leave with all the ministers in the church: May the grace of the Lord Jesus Christ, and the love of God, and the fellowship of the Holy Spirit be with you all.

24 Reformation Ministry

Are You Being Reformed by the Word of God?

Revival is a work of God's Holy Spirit, but it shows itself through the vitality and renewal of what Jonathan Edwards calls "Religious Affections." He describes revival as a "renewed interest in the things of religion [and a] vigorous upsurge of revivalism at the level of personal religion." Revival is not theoretical. It is an experience, not emotionalism, even though the emotions are affected, but more importantly the religious experience is visible and believable. The manifestation of these criteria seem to be absent among the majority of evangelicals at the beginning of this century. Why is there no revival in the evangelical church?

Reformation (the recovery of biblical truth) will always precede revival. First, one must acknowledge the authority of Scripture. The central teaching of Scripture states that a right standing with God comes by faith alone and that faith itself is a gift of God, as salvation itself is a gift from God. What is the primary means for announcing this gift from God? The primary means is preaching the Word of God and preaching is the instrument of reformation and revival.

Richard Hofstadter in his Pulitzer Prize winning book, *Anti-Intellectualism in American Life*, points out that "sermons are not producing any noticeable change in the lives of Christians in North America." In comparing sermons today with the sermons preached 200 years ago in this country Hofstadter posits, "Puritan sermons combined philosophy, piety, and scholarship... . The clergy assumed responsibility for a literate culture. Such an assumption shows the gulf between the profound substance of Puritan sermons and some of the modern inspirational pep talks which pass for sermons."

Preaching has moved from substantial reflections on the character and nature of God to a forum on "How to...do things, have things, and be successful." The "How to Gospel" has bankrupted the evangelical church. The biblical gospel is almost extinct and is certainly offensive to the ears of most evangelicals.

"We are accused of rash and impious innovation, for having ventured to propose any change at all on the former state of the Church" (The Necessity of Reforming the Church, by John Calvin, Works, vol. 1, p.125). Calvin used two interesting words that aptly describe reformation. The word "innovation" from the Latin word *innovare*, which means "to renew," was needed in the day of Calvin and it is needed today. The church does not need a new gospel or a new way to worship, but it does need to restore the gospel and the orthodox way to worship which has been trampled upon over the past couple of centuries. Innovation describes the work of reformation and change describes the result of reformation.

Michael Horton argues that "theology, not morality, is the first business on the church's agenda of reform, and the church, not society, is the first target of divine criticism" (*Beyond Culture Wars*). Innovation begins with theology and ends with theology. Paul the apostle said, "I press on to take hold of that for which Christ Jesus took hold of me." Paul strived for an understanding of righteousness, peace and the knowledge of Jesus Christ, which is essentially and practically theological. Paul's innovation rested squarely on a theological framework. A reformer is innovative only when he or she has a passion for believing and living according to God's standard as he or she is enabled to believe and live by the power of the Holy Spirit.

The meaning of reformation and thus what it means to be a reforming Christian, has been forgotten, because the evangelical church, the carrier of reformation, has turned her back on the foundational doctrines of the Christian faith. True reformation is the church being reformed by the Word of God. The evangelical church has replaced the law and the gospel with human-centered structures that meet "felt needs," those that are "user-friendly", and are "seeker sensitive."

At the beginning of the 16th century Reformation Martin of Basle came to the knowledge of the truth of the gospel, but he was afraid to make a public confession. He wrote these words on a leaf of parchment: "O most merciful Christ, I know that I can be saved only by the merit of thy blood. Holy Jesus, I acknowledge thy sufferings for me. I love thee! I love thee!" He removed a stone from the wall of his chamber and hid it. It was not discovered until a hundred years later.

About the same time Martin Luther discovered the truth and he openly confessed: "My Lord has confessed me before men; I will not shrink from confessing Him before kings." The Reformation continued and we remember Martin Luther for his devotion to innovation and change, but what about Martin of Basle? Who was the reformer?

Innovation is that aspect of reformation that seeks to recover the integrity and dignity of the Christian religion. Our forefathers suffered and died for the integrity of the gospel and with dignity they have passed on to us the torch of reformation. John Calvin left the church with these words and I leave them with you.

> But be the issue what it may, we will never repent of having begun and of having proceeded thus far... We will die, but in death even be conquerors...because we know that our blood will be as seed to propagate the Divine truth which men now despise" (*The Necessity of Reforming the Church*, by John Calvin, Vol. 1, p. 234.)

Hope and Vision for Reformation

Thomas Edison said that "restlessness and discontent are the first necessities of progress." I find myself restless and discontent with the obvious decline of the true Christian religion as it is defined by the Word of God. My restless and discontent soul drives me to ask myself the question: Martin, do you have a vision and hope for reformation in the church?

If you think I have a passion for reformation, then I'm guilty. My passion is not for the return of the 16th century Reformation or the return of the "good ole days" (which were not good at all). My passion is for reformation with a little "r." Our 16th century Reformation forefathers were not satisfied with the Reformation, they wanted reformation. They understood the biblical concept of reformation, which demands the recovery or discovery of biblical truth. The recovery of the law and gospel is the foundation for reformation in the church. The Reformation fathers were God's instruments to recover the truth from the whole counsel of God. They saw reformation as an indicative in the present tense and in the passive voice. It was a matter of fact "they were being reformed." They were active participants, but they were being acted upon by the Holy Spirit and the Word of God.

This brings the church to a point of self-examination. Is the church being reformed by the Word of God through the illuminating power of the Holy Spirit or does the church try to reform the Word of God according the power of darkness? The evidence indicates a strong move among reformed and evangelical churches toward reforming the Word of God rather than being reformed by it.

The cause of the epidemic abuse cannot be easily traced to any particular discipline or lack thereof. However, there are several foundational philosophical dynamics at work. When the 16th century Reformation began, the parochialism of Rome was replaced by evangelicalism, which is truly universal. While the church was liberated from parochialism, there was the sacrifice of unity for diversity. Although diversity is not sinful in essence, it affords the opportunity for the birth and nurture for private agendas and ultimately individualism.

The cultural milieu has been and still is in the process of change. The light of modernity begins to fade as postmodern thinkers begin to emerge. Orthodox belief systems are being challenged. Historical Revisionism and deconstructionism have trickled down from the intellectual elites to the rest of us. Theology has been replaced with religion. Intellectual pursuit has been replaced with the "dumbing down of Christians." Sacrifice has been replaced by prosperity seekers. Tradition has been replaced by the contemporary. Tradition may become sin, but it is not essentially and necessarily sinful. Tradition is important to provide stability to an orthodox belief system.

Christians rightly ask, "What's the solution?" The solution is a process called reformation. The Word of God rather than our preferences must be the basis of our belief system. Confessional standards must be maintained with integrity and dignity. A passion for truth must find a place of honor at the debate table. The aggregate of these principles equals reformation in the church.

What we believe, what we know, and what we practice will set the agenda for reformation in the church. On the other hand corruption and a continuing descent away from biblical truth will steal away the hope and vision for reformation. It is my hope and vision that pastors, theologians, and laymen will find a passion for reformation in their individual soul. The expression of that passion will be the seed for revival in the church.

The mandate to carry the gospel to the ends of the earth is abundantly clear in Scripture. However, in recent church history men have devised many pragmatic schemes to "win the lost." The side show mentality has found its way into the church with astounding success and with it a plan for people to make a decision for Christ. Now I ask you, with all the evangelistic success over the past 100 years, why is the church so sick? The answer is simple. The powers to be in the church failed to teach reformation principles, thus they forgot to recover the truth of the law and gospel. The gospel went forth without the law. A sinner cannot believe and receive the gospel without the law preceding the gospel. An appreciation of God's grace can be seen only in the light of God's wrath. Remove God's wrath and the gospel is worthless. The hope and vision for reformation will give the church hope and vision for making disciples and a new order for personal Christian growth.

It is time for reforming reformers to step forward and tell the local church that the church must be reformed by the Word of God. You may be the one person who will inspire the congregation with the spirit of reformation. It is my prayer that your hope and vision for the church is reformation. If you've read this book and believe I'm wrong, please explain my error. Even so, I still have hope and vision for the church being reformed according to the Word of God, by the power of the Holy Spirit.

Reformation Precedes Revival

Many professing Christians are pro-relativism, pro-pragmatism, pro-secular-psychological-therapy, pro-management, pro-Arminian, and pro-higher criticism, just to mention a few of the elements that cause me to say professing. Professing Church leaders and their followers are inclined to man-made religious ideas rather than teaching the whole counsel of God. Ecumenical colloquium has replaced church councils. Doctrinal purity is despised. It makes me wonder if the greater part of evangelical Christianity is in the clutches of apostasy without even knowing it or if it is known, it is suppressed. The sadder and more painful effect of all these and innumerable other ungodly religious movements falls on the man in the pew. Week by week his mind is filled with false doctrine. His world and life view slowly develops until he finally adopts an apostate world and life view. It may take several generations, but sooner or later truth, honor, and dignity will take leave from the visible evangelical church. I fear that time has arrived and now reformation must be our goal. It is true that there are pockets of reformation at one place or the other in the church.

October 31, 1517 is a special day in church history. It was on this day that Martin Luther challenged the church with his 95 theses. Luther never intended to start a new church or to divide the Roman Catholic Church. Luther simply wanted to see reform within the church. He saw the condition of the church and wanted to debate some theological issues that were un-orthodox for Christianity. Although others paved the way before him, most historians credit October 31, 1517 as the beginning of the Protestant Reformation. The Protestant Church was a product of the 16th century Reformation in Europe.

By the end of the 20th century, the Protestant Church had lost its meaning and purpose. The word protestant is derived from the Latin word *protestari*, which has the root meaning "to protest." James Davidson Hunter, Professor of Sociology and Religious Studies at the University of Virginia, correctly assessed the historical perspective. He said that "the Protestant Reformation in the 16th century created one of the most fundamental cultural divisions in the history of Western Civilization." He goes on to say, "the practical efforts of the Reformation have, at least in the U.S. context, become both politically and culturally defunct." The protestant church is no longer protesting against the ungodly world and life views that prevail within the halls of evangelicalism.

Martin Luther protested against the deviation from the fundamental teachings of Christianity. He argued that the church must return to the doctrine of *sola fide* (faith alone). Sola fide teaches that man is *declared righteous* in the sight of God by an act of God. The contrary heresy was that man was *made righteous*, a prevailing doctrine in the modern evangelical church. The authority by which Luther would argue for the doctrine of "justification by faith alone" was *sola scriptura* (by Scripture alone). Luther realized that Holy Scripture is the ultimate authority for the church. From these "protests" (by faith alone, by Scripture alone, and others) the Protestant Church was born.

Since reformation is the subject of our discussion, let me define a couple of terms before I continue:

1. Reformation - the recovery (or discovery) of biblical truth
2. Revival - the practice of biblical truth after it has been recovered or discovered

When God sends reformation some will embrace it and others will hate it. "At a time when God manifests himself in such a great work for his church, there is no such thing as being neuter." This statement may be found in an essay written by Jonathan Edwards during the time of reformation and revival at his church in Northampton, Mass. Jesus said, "He who is not with Me is against Me" (Luke 11:23).

When God sent the angels to Sodom to warn Lot of the impending judgment, Lot warned the unreformed men, but they ignored Lot. The minds of the wicked men of Sodom simply could not be reformed. Why did those wicked men not experience the kind of reformation and revival that Jonathan Edwards saw at Northampton? There may be different reasons.

One of the primary reasons for the absence of reformation is ignorance. Reformation and revival will never proceed from those who have never been shown the truth from the Bible. Then there are those who have been shown the truth, but they refuse to embrace the truth. If professing Christians have no concern or interest in truth, then the Spirit of God may not reside in their souls. Obviously reformation cannot take place if people are unconcerned about truth.

Disinterest in truth, reformation, and revival should be a grave concern to the church. The church that is not reforming will devolve its corruption to the next generation. Sooner or later the church will become so corrupt it will be called *Ichabod* (the glory has departed from Israel). If professing Christians have no concern or interest for truth, then the Spirit of God may be absent from those souls. If the Spirit of God is absent, then there cannot be reformation. If there is no reformation (re-discovery of biblical truth), then there cannot be a revival. True biblical reformation will always precede revival. If revival is the first order of business, the result is a false man-made salvation or people seeking to earn salvation by their moral choices. If Christ is our Savior then our salvation is not man-made, but quite on the contrary our salvation is God-made. If Christ is our Lord then we seek to please Him in all our moral choices, rather than making moral choices to please ourselves.

It is an error to think that biblical reformation is a concept discovered by Martin Luther 500 years ago on October 31st. "What Luther did was to rediscover vital Christianity and to give it afresh to the world" (*The Works of B. B. Warfield*, Vol. 9, p. 463).

Biblical reformation is just that – it is biblical. Our reformation forefathers simply recovered and practiced the long forgotten concept that "the church reformed is always being reformed." Remember, a church that is not being reformed by the Word of God will devolve its corruption to the next generation.

The 17th century Puritan, Francis Turretin, said the call to reformation is such that "a man is bound to purge his faith and worship of all the errors and superstitions by which it could be corrupted so that he may retain religion pure from every stain" (*Elenctic Theology*, vol. 3, p. 217). Is it possible for a man to purge his faith and worship of all errors and superstitions? Is it possible to remove all the corruption that comes from the sinful heart? Is it possible for our religion to be pure from every stain? The challenge is great and only possible if we are always being reformed by the Word of God. The Bible instructs us how we may remove all the corruption that comes from the sinful heart. Our religion will never be completely pure from every stain, but if there is any purity at all, it will be the result of reformation. Are we willing to work for the recovery of biblical truth?

There is an axiom that says "if you don't use it, you lose it." If we apply that to the concept of reformation, we must say that if we don't use the Word of God, we will lose the Word of God. In this materialist and consumeristic age one may argue that the Word of God is in abundance. Everyone has one, two, or maybe even five Bibles in the house. If you visit the bookstore you will find the youth Bible, the serendipity Bible, the boys Bible, the girls Bible and a whole host of Bibles to accommodate most any need you might have. Even so, I say we are in danger of losing the Bible for several different reasons:

1. It is possible to lose the Word of God because of indifference.
2. It is possible to lose the Word of God because the Scriptures are not studied.
3. If the preaching of the Word of God is despised, then the Word of God may be lost.
4. It is possible to lose the Word of God because it is considered irrelevant.

Many professing Christians are indifferent toward the Word of God and some of them, strange as it may seem, attach little importance to the Word of God. Then there is an equal number who simply do not study the Word of God. Whether we lose the Word of God through neglect, misbelief, or disobedience, we are brought to the same end. Sin, vice, and misery are the natural results of losing the Word of God. Without the Word of God, men and women will hate true worship. Without the Word of God false worship will replace true worship. So without the Word of God the church has no purpose.

A brief study of church history will reveal that the Bible has been lost to a lesser or greater degree at certain times and places in every period of the history of the church. The question we must ask is: What about today? The church as a whole is in a sad state. Survey after survey reveals that many if not most professing Christians can't even name the Ten Commandments. Although they may use popular or even orthodox religious language, many have little understanding of salvation through grace by faith in Christ alone. Practice does not precede knowledge, despite the assertions made by religious professors. You must know something before you can believe something and you must believe something before you can practice something.

When the Holy Spirit has done His work and changes the hearts of His people, then being reformed by the Word of God will continue throughout their lives. Being reformed by the Word of God will touch every part of your soul – the mind, the emotions, the will. Once a child of God discovers the law and the gospel intellectually and emotionally it will have an effect on his or her decisions. There will be an outward manifestation of his or her love for truth. Being reformed by the Word of God is a necessary principle that must not be avoided by the church.

Recovering the law and the gospel is ultimately important. We cannot put it off any longer! What will we devolve on the shoulders of the next generation if we do not seriously seek reformation in the church, thus affecting every area of life including our religious, familial, social, economic, and political lives. To defer reformation to another person or another time is dangerous indeed, because such thinking and actions will surely provoke God's wrath. There is a choice: reformation or judgment!

After Jonah experienced personal reformation he took the reformation to Nineveh. The Word of God says Jonah preached a sermon that went something like this: "Yet forty days, and Nineveh shall be overthrown" (Jonah 3:4). Apparently Jonah's preaching was very powerful, because the whole city repented in sackcloth and ashes. How wonderful to see the universal nature of reformation that was occasioned by their faith in God. How wonderful to see the reformation move from city streets to the palace, from the common man to the heads of state. The undeniable truth from the book of Jonah is that the reformation at Nineveh saved that city from God's impending judgment, unlike the city of Sodom.

God's warnings are all around us. In the church, out of the church and throughout the natural world, God sends His warnings. True ministers of the Word of God who preach the full counsel of God are instruments of God to warn all people of God's coming judgment (please read Ezekiel 33:1-11). Reformation is absolutely necessary for the church and culture!

Demythologize the Church

Jesus mentioned the church a few times in the New Testament, but He didn't devote a chapter to define the nature, purpose, mission, and ministry of the church. However, Jesus left the church this promise: "I will build my church" (Matthew 16:18). The word *church* found in the New Testament has been misused and misinterpreted throughout the history of the church. It is my purpose to share some thoughts on the nature of the church. The great challenge is to demythologize the church. This brief list will help:

The church is not someplace you go to.

The church is not a building.

The church is not an institution.

The church is not owned by anyone on this planet.

The church is not graded by ethnicity, importance, or social status.

The church is not divided by doctrine.

What is the church? Hold on to your hat because the answer is simple, but it will blow you away. The church is the people of God. Christians living in a specific geographical area gather together as a local congregation to fulfill the purpose, mission, and ministry of the church. Specifically, but not limited to: collective worship according to the Word of God, preaching, teaching, fellowship, and prayer.

The church is not singularly identified. It is embodied within two dimensions commonly known as the visible church and the invisible church

The church visible is mixed with wheat and tares. One prominent church creed describes the visible church as the whole "number of professing Christians, with their children, associated together for divine worship and godly living, agreeable to the Scriptures and submitting to the lawful government of Christ's kingdom."

The church invisible is the church in heaven. The invisible church is the true church or to put it another way the saved church. The invisible church is infallible, indestructible, indivisible, and universal.

The Bible does not have a specific proof text to prove the nature of the church. The full counsel of God must be consulted to discover the nature of the church. The Bible does use metaphors to describe the nature of the church. A metaphor is a figure of speech that draws a comparison between two things. The comparison is not literally expressed and may be understood by implication. Although space does not permit inquiry into all the biblical metaphors a few of them will suffice.

The first metaphor I bring to your attention is the vineyard (Matthew 21:33-46; John 15:1-8). The nature of the vineyard is such that it is productive. Likewise the church is productive when it fulfills the responsibilities given to the church according to the Word of God. The preaching of the Word of God has been given to the church. When the church insures the sound preaching of the Word of God, it is productive.

The field is another metaphor that will help us understand the nature of the church. The field belongs to God; the church is the field, therefore God's people belong to Him (1 Corinthians 3:5-9).

The Bible also uses another agricultural metaphor to describe the nature of the church. That metaphor found often in the gospel of John is a flock (John 10:1-16). Raising sheep was common in all ancient Near Eastern cultures. Sheep provided food, clothing, and sacrifices for religious worship. Sheep need a shepherd to feed them and protect them. The shepherd in the local church is the pastor/elder. The sheep/shepherd metaphor was a favorite of the Lord Jesus Christ. Obviously the sheep/shepherd aspect ultimately has the invisible church in mind.

One of my favorite metaphors used to describe the nature of the church is the family of God (Luke 11:13; Romans 8:14-17; Galatians 4:5-7). The nature of the church is such that order, harmony, and unity are necessary for each local congregation. The modern notion that families function best when the various parties are disaffected, is one reason that local congregations feud, fight, and divide. If children in the family can't get along, neither can siblings in the family of God.

The Bible also describes the church as a bride (Ephesians 5:22-29). The biblical bride is supposed to be pure, and so it is with the church. The biblical bride submits to, honors, and obeys the groom. The nature of the church found in the biblical bride should show us the inseparable connection of God to His bride, the church.

Given the biblical teaching on the nature of the church what does Jesus mean when he said, "I will build my church." Does the Lord mean that he would build a physical building? Many professing Christians think of the church in terms of a physical piece of architecture. The physical structures where professing Christians meet for worship, Bible study, and fellowship have become a synonym for the church. The result is a misunderstanding of the nature of the church.

The church is God's building according to the Word of God. One verse from the Bible will make the point: "And what agreement has the temple of God with idols? For you are the temple of the living God. As God has said: I will dwell in them and walk among them. I will be their God and they shall be My people" (2 Corinthians. 6:16). The church in biblical terms is not a building made by men, but rather a building created in the image of God. Notice the rhetorical question asked by the inspired apostle: "What agreement has the temple of God with idols?" None of course! God is true! An idol is false! Only truth is acceptable in God's building. Falsehood and lies are unacceptable.

God's building consists of the souls of Christians filled with the Holy Spirit of God. If Christians would come to grips with the nature of the church maybe the seeds of revival will germinate into beautiful plants. Many Christians do not understand the nature of the church. Several generations grew up under a subjective set of rules that did not include a proper understanding of the fundamental principles that would have taken them down a different road.

The church in the south more than any part of the country has traditionally served as the center of social and cultural functions, thus associating the church with a building. It was the building that provided entertainment to the body rather than enrichment to the soul. The church in the Bible belt has been treated like a social club, civic club, country club, men's club, and women's club.

Christians must set aside the baggage from previous generations. It is hard to set aside old habits, but Christians should reconsider the nature of the church and re-examine what the Bible says about the nature of the church. The church has been abused, used, and amused through the centuries. Set aside the traditional views of the church and adopt the dynamic views as you find them in the Word of God. Set your goal to demythologize the church for coming generations.

About the Authors

Pastor James Vickery was a servant of the Lord. He began to pastor God's people at an early age and for years has sought to encourage, edify and build the kingdom of God. Those that know him can attest to his dedication and efforts to grow and bless the work of the Lord. Except for the time he took to further his education, he constantly served as a pastor. Whether he had to work a secular job and pastor or just pastor, he has been faithful to the call he received at a young age.

Martin Murphy has a B.A. in Bible from Columbia International University and Master of Divinity from Reformed Theological Seminary. Martin spent nearly thirty years in the class room, the pulpit, the lectern, the study, and the library. He now devotes most of his time consolidating academic and practical gains by writing books. He and his wife Mary live in Dothan, Alabama. He is the author of fourteen Christian books.

www.ingramcontent.com/pod-product-compliance
Lightning Source LLC
Chambersburg PA
CBHW071506040426
42444CB00008B/1519